WHATEVER

Mike J. Aronson

ISBN 978-1-63630-749-7 (Paperback)
ISBN 978-1-63630-750-3 (Digital)

Stickmen figures illustrated by Lee Nicholas

Covenant Books, Inc.
11661 Hwy 707
Murrells Inlet, SC 29576
www.covenantbooks.com

That man is a success who has lived well, laughed often and loved much; who has gained the respect of intelligent women and men and the love of children who never lacks appreciation of the earth's beauty or fails to express it; who follows his dreams and pursues excellence in each task; and who brings out the best in others; and gives only the best of himself. (Eulogy for Frank Torina, February 5, 2009)

I dedicate this book to my lifelong friend, Frank Torina. Frank was the master at *Whatever*. He was always so quick with a joke and some very perinate statements, always smiling and always looking out for the betterment of others.

Frank, I love you. You were so well blessed by so many other lives you have touched! RIP.

Keynote

*W*hatever will inspire you to make your life better. *Whatever* will inspire you to help others. *Whatever* will bring you a lot of smiles and laughs, and you will say to yourself, "I didn't know that! Oh, is that so? Now that's funny!"

Preface

If Jerry Seinfeld can have a show about nothing and Kramer can write a coffee-table book that turns into a coffee table, I can write a book about WHATEVER!

I am not a writer, and I am not a reader. I know I have missed so much in my career of life by not being a reader. On the other side, I guess I was doing something else instead of reading. I must have been doing something. But even doing nothing is something. I am just a regular Joe getting though this life that we live. I do have an empathetic attitude toward people or at least most people. I feel once we realize in this world that we live in that we are just people helping people. I tell this to my granddaughter, age seven, and now she often repeats back to me, "Granddaddy, sometimes people just may need some help." I tell this to my granddaughter a lot, and now she repeats it back to me: at times, some people may need some help. It is the little things that matter, like when we take out the trash to make sure we place the can in a proper spot so the garbageman can get it easily and be able to do his job and help someone when in traffic and at least give them a wave of thanks. And if they don't help you out or cut you off, as Jimmy Buffett said, "I didn't get mad, I just wrote song about them." One of his unknown best that says so much.

"You were born an a——hole."

The list goes on and on.

WHATEVER is out there, you just have to embrace it whenever you see or hear it and make it work for you!!!!

Remember that your job can affect someone else's job. What it comes down to it, everyone doesn't think the same. Can you believe sometimes what other people do and what could they be thinking? But they do. You feel sorry for them, and a lot of times, you have seen these types of people and they don't even feel sorry for themselves. I wasn't born to raise you.

Yes, I know some people are mentally disturbed and have a sickness or a chemical imbalance of some sort. You feel sorry for them, and a lot of times, you have seen these types of people, and they don't even feel sorry for themselves.

If we all think the same, that would not be good either. What an influence we all have on others, especially the young.

We are the people our parents warned us about. Everything we learned we learned in kindergarten—sharing, saying "please" and "thank you," not hurting anyone, helping out others; the list goes on and on.

Sometimes people just need some help.

That is the purpose of this book, to help yourself and for you to help someone else. Also to have a few laughs and smiles along the way.

Oh no. You're saying, "Here is another motivational book."

Not!!!!

All I am hoping for is that when you read this book, something that you have read will change you for the better or more importantly, help you to make something better for someone else.

If you think this is all a bunch of crap, great. Just take the book back and get a refund. Or possibly let me know and I will refund your money. Or just donate it or recycle it or just throw it away. Could also make a great drink coaster.

Yes, all the quotes, sayings, and words in this book, I could have just gotten off the internet. But I didn't. Yes, I did see things on internet because the internet and social media are everywhere, and you just have to identify it. Anyone could have written this book, but they didn't, and I have.

All of these quotes and pictures I recorded from my everyday work and play experiences. I knew at the time they were positive thoughts, inspirational, and at times, some were just funny. I wanted to record them so I could pass them on to you. I have no intent to plagiarize or take away from the author of the quotes or whom the quotes are credited to. I just want to spread their ideas and thoughts using another method.

Whatever is an accumulation of over twenty years and really a lifetime of observations, situations, experiences, and opinions that I have witnessed and experienced.

Yep, opinions are like a——holes. Everyone has one. Did I miss things? Yep. Did I repeat stuff? Probably. Is there more out there that I could have included? Yes, every day and everywhere. You just have to recognize it and use it. Should we maybe adopt Kramer's idea on Seinfeld and all of us wear name badges so we can call each other by name and maybe relate to each other better? Maybe so, but at the speed we are going, we will all soon have a computer chip and a bar code on our foreheads anyway.

Will I write more? Maybe. This book has no end, but I had to stop somewhere. I know when I do stop. I will remember or experience something or see something that I should have written in this book. Now I challenge you to see something or experience something that should be in the book. And you will make your own book.

But *Whatever* is mostly used when one cannot come up with an answer or when they feel they cannot control something or they do not know what to say. So they just shrug their shoulders and say "*Whatever!*"

This book has no chapters and no real organization or flow. If there was, it would not be *Whatever.*

According to the Huffington Post in 2013, the casual *Whatever* was rated the most annoying word by 38% of the 1,173 adults surveyed. And in 2015, the most annoying word or phrase in casual conversation is *Whatever,* according to the Marist College annual poll. Yes, I did look this up on the internet.

Even George Stephanopoulos of *Good Morning America* feels the same way about *Whatever.* Chis Collinsworth said *Whatever* three times in two sentences while working his *Sunday Night Football* broadcast. He may have been at a loss for words.

Whatever can be used in so many ways as a pronoun, adverb, verb, etc. or even a cop-out to end a statement when you are at a loss for words, as an exclamation to an idea. When you have nothing more to say, when you can't think of what to say or how to say it, as a negative but also as a positive, depending how and when you use the word, you can use *Whatever*. You may make someone mad, but you could make them happy as you agree to *Whatever* they say.

How many times in a day do you hear the word *Whatever*? Several times. At times, I have hashed marked throughout the day each time I heard the word just throughout my regular workday. Sometimes as many as ten to fifteen times in a day.

When we are watching TV or movies, it is used all the time and written into the scripts or just casually said by someone.

Do not take advantage of *Whatever*. Say it to your advantage and use it wisely. Respect the word.

Yes, too many times it is taken as a negative statement in itself. But *Whatever* is *Whatever*, and there is no right or wrong, just the way it is said or meant to be said or the way it is interpreted or meant to be interpreted.

In the following pages, you will see that *Whatever* is out there to be seen and heard and however we interpret it. I hope you take it in the way it was intended it to be, that is, in a positive manner, helping yourself and helping each other. And of course, smile and laugh.

These quotes, sayings, pictures, etc. are all over Facebook, Instagram, Twitter, articles, newspapers, and all kinds of communications. The problem is, we see them and read them all the time, but we just don't do anything with them, just like all the pictures that you have on your phone. Do you do anything with them? Or do you just scroll through them trying to find a picture from two years ago? Do something with them. Blow them up and frame them. If you give someone a picture, great, but if you frame it and give it to them, they almost have a commitment to display it somewhere to remember it, or the picture just becomes just a memory in the corner of their mind.

But when you buy a new phone, you have to make sure all your pictures will get transferred even if they just stay on your phone, then you will have more stuff to do nothing with. A lot is out there for us to make good use of our pictures. Look at all the websites and places you can go to put your pictures out there and remember them better. Calendars, mugs, books, wall art, etcetera, etcetera.

Sorry. I was on a picture rant.

So I decided to capture *Whatever* and compile and record them and now share *Whatever* with you. Hopefully you will do the same and share the positives with someone else and make their future better. And if it is negative, turn it around into a positive.

Am I positive all the time? Hell no. I'm human. Do I try to be? Maybe most of the time. It is an attitude you take and what you decide to do with it. You never hear coaches telling their team to go out there and be negative, to give up, not to try. Will it always turn out the way you want it to? Nope! You may not always get the answer you wanted to hear, but it is the answer. And it may make you feel better also.

I do not believe that winning is the only thing and that winning is everything. I dislike some of the phrases like "Second place is the first loser" and "Winning is the only thing." I guess in some cases that is true, like, if your job or livelihood depends on it. But if you win, then that means someone else loses, and that is not good for them. Oh yes, unless you're in Vegas. Yes, nobody really likes to lose, I know that. But if you don't lose, how do you know what it is like to win? The important thing is that you were able to play, to participate and engage. Try to do your best and give a good effort in *Whatever* you do. If you don't win, you will still feel better that you tried and that you gave it your best. This book is not intended to hurt, degrade, pick on, scam, punk, beat up, be politically correct, rub the wrong way, punish, or even piss you off. But at times it might. It is intended to be what it is—*Whatever*. Accept it for that and enjoy. If you don't enjoy it, maybe you need to go back and read something again, as you may have missed it. You won't agree with everything and that's okay. I don't either, but I put it out there so you could have a choice. All these quotes, sayings, passages, poems, writings, pictures—or even at times BS—are not meant to steal from the writer or to take advantage of or hurt anyone. By recognizing *Whatever*, you will be able to help yourself and help others. And more you can gain from it.

I know I have missed so much that is out there. And there is so more out there every day. Many people express themselves in many ways with a song or in a movie or in a book, writing how they feel and how they feel about others. As Garth Brooks noted, to recognize the writers of the songs as well as the performers. The performer is a vehicle getting the words and message out there as the writer intended. There are so many great lines in songs and movies that it would be impossible to capture them all. Now it is up to you to find them and embrace them. Definitely things that we all can relate to.

The word *Whatever*, as defined by *Merriam Webster*, means "anything or everything that," "no matter what," "regardless of what," "used in questions that express surprise or confusion."

I hope you enjoy this book and it helps you to become a better person. But even better, I hope that it helps you help someone else. If this happens for you, then I have accomplished my task. If not, maybe take a look at yourself, and see if there is possibly a reason why. If not, *Whatever!* I wasn't born to raise you.

Whatever is out there, you just have to find it and embrace it. Whenever you see or hear it and make it work for you, carry on.

Whatever

Everybody's got their "stuff" about stuff.

To quote one of the greats, George Carlin, "move your shit so I can put my stuff there."

Stuff can be material things, but mainly it's mental. How do you deal with your stuff? Deal with your stuff in a positive way. If it is negative stuff, then turn it around into a positive and learn from it. Don't create more negative stuff. Lean more toward the positive stuff. Druggies usually hang around other druggies. Remember, negative people hang around negative people. Positive people hang around positive people. Negativity spreads like a disease, but also positive attitudes can also spread like a disease. Hits bring on more hits in baseball as well as in life. The old saying tells us that if you give someone a smile, they will smile back. If you have a positive attitude toward stuff, your stuff won't turn into "shit." And this can be a positive for you. Other people's shit will turn into stuff, and then you might be able to help them with their stuff and not their shit.

Have a nice day.

"Shit happens," but you can make stuff happen.

Swing hard you may hit it.

SHIT. Ship High in Transit.

Sometimes it's not where you are now. It's where you want to be in twenty minutes! At times, it's not where you want to go to sleep but rather where you want to wake up.

Happiness is not the absence of stress. It's the ability to cope with it.

"Pain Is Temporary, Pride Is Forever," a song by Don Diablo.

Stack them high and let them fly.

Meetings are up and sales are down.

*****

Jake: Do you want some cake?
Millie: I don't eat sugar.
Jake: Yeah, me either unless it's in, like, pies and cakes and stuff.
Millie: *Whatever.*
Jake: Yeah, *Whatever.*

Alan: As opposed to a set menu or buffet style.
Charlie: Sure, *Whatever.*

Did you get a haircut?
No, I got them all cut.
Yeah, *Whatever*, how many times have you heard that?

*****

When you use the word *Whatever*, it can be derogatory or flattering. Well, maybe not flattering but not derogatory either, depending on the way you use it. Not to mention your tone of voice or your gestures. You should not prepare for *Whatever*. It just should flow from your speech in a natural way. DO NOT abuse the word, but on the other side, say it with dignity so you can express your true meaning.

Pickup lines:
Do you believe in the hereafter? Because if you're not here for what I am here after, then you will still be here after I am gone.

WHATEVER

When I was talking to you, everyone else in the room just faded away. Yeah, *Whatever!*

*****

Life without passion, you're dead.
>—Shire Schmidt

Nice body, but she has a BUTTERFACE. BUT-HER-FACE

Did you hear the one about the campfire girl who fell in the fire and came out a brownie?

A guy walks into a bar, a second guy walks into a bar, the third guy ducks.

Life is 10% what happens to me and 90% how I react to it.
>—Charles Swindoll

Management is 90% people skills and 10% knowing your job.
>—Unknown

They could have been 5–0 or *Whatever*.
>—Joe Morgan

I don't know Karate, but I know crazy, and I'm not afraid to use it.
>—James Bond

Whatever, I want to talk to my lawyer.
>—*The Mentalist*

Whatever we won! Chill out. Good Lord.
—Sugar to Randy, *Survivor*

Once you let your grief become anger, it will never go away…
—*Lost*

My Father's Day present from my daughter was another year of not having to pay for a wedding.

One guy's fantasy is another guy's lunch.
For every good-looking woman, there is another man sick of her.

Sometimes it is better to beg for forgiveness, than to ask for permission.

If you don't like change, then you are going to watch.

*****

Ask the next question such as "Where is the subway station?" "Which way are you going, uptown or downtown?" This is a good example that, at times, we should ask the next question for clarification, such as the example with "Where is the subway question?" Not only do you need to where the subway is; you need to know which way you are headed so as not to go down the wrong steps ending up on the wrong sides of the tracks.

You don't need to be faster than the bear. You just need to be faster than your friend.

What is your favorite place to go?
It is the next place I go to.

The entrepreneur always searches for change, responds to it, and exploits it as an opportunity.

Old aunts used to come up to me at weddings, poking me in the ribs and crackling, telling me, "You're next."

They stopped after I started doing the same thing to them at funerals.

Life is like a roll of toilet paper. The closer you get to the end, the faster it goes, so have fun. "Good thoughts only," learn to laugh at yourself, and count your blessings.

*****

Rudeness is the weak man's imitation of strength.
—Eric Hoffer

National Parks now embrace the idea of America itself.
—Abe Lincoln

True terror is to wake up one morning and discover that your high school class is running the country.
—Kurt Vonnegut

Most smiles are started by another smile.
Most yawns are started by another yawn.
—Roger Staubach

Sometimes we don't get to choose what happens to us but we do get to choose what we do about it.

TODAY

*Outside my window, a new day I see
and only I can determine, what kind of day it will be.
It can be busy and sunny, laughing and gay,
or be boring and cold, unhappy and grey.
My own state of mind is the determining key,
for I am the only person I let myself be.
I can be thoughtful and do all I can to help,
or be selfish and think just of myself.
I can enjoy when I make it seem fun,
or gripe and complain and make it hard on someone.
I can be patient with those who do not understand,
or belittle and hurt them as much as I can.
But I have faith in myself,
and I believe what I say,
and I personally intend to make
the best of each day.*

Jan LaValley

The man who fears not truth has nothing to fear from lies.

—Thomas Jefferson

I only regret that I have but one life to lose for my country.

—Nathan Hale

Let us tenderly and kindly cherish, therefore, the means of knowledge. Let us dare to read, think, speak and write.

—John Adams

Historical Trivia

Did you know the saying "God willing and the Creeks don't rise" was in reference to the Creek Indians and not a body of water? It was written by Benjamin Hawkins in the late eighteenth century. He was a politician and an Indian diplomat. While in the south, Hawkins was requested by the president of the US to return to Washington. In his response, he was said to have written, "God willing and the Creeks don't rise." Because he capitalized the word *creeks*, it is deduced that he was referring to the Creek Indian tribe and not a body of water.

*****

In George Washington's days, there were no cameras. One's image was either sculpted or painted. Some paintings of George Washington showed him standing behind a desk with one arm behind his back while others showed both legs and both arms. Prices charged by painters were not based on how many people were to be painted but by how many limbs were to be painted. Arms and legs are limbs; therefore, painting them would cost the buyer more. Hence the expression, "Okay, but it'll cost you an arm and a leg." (Artists know hands and arms are more difficult to paint.) This really came to light for me on a visit to the Vatican. Seeing all the sculptors and artwork and rugs, it was amazing. Then to find out at times not one person completed the rug or the sculpture. People were specialists at their crafts. So, if you needed a finger made or painted you could call

Herb, and if you need a hand then call Eddie, or Joe or Sam. So if you needed a hand or a finger, just call Herb or call Eddie.

*****

As incredible as it sounds, men and women took baths only twice a year (May and October). Women kept their hair covered while men shaved their heads (because of lice and bugs) and wore wigs. Wealthy men could afford good wigs made from wool. They couldn't wash the wigs, so to clean them, they would carve out a loaf of bread, put the wig in the shell, and bake it for thirty minutes. The heat would make the wig big and fluffy, hence the term "big wig." Today we often use the idiom "Here comes the big wig" because someone appears to be or is powerful and wealthy.

*****

In the late 1700s, many houses consisted of a large room with only one chair, which was commonly a long, wide board folded down from the wall and was used for dining. The head of the household always sat in the chair while everyone else ate sitting on the floor. Occasionally a guest, who was usually a man, would be invited to sit in this chair during a meal. To sit in the chair meant you were important and in charge. They called the one sitting in the chair the "chair man." Today in business, we use the expression or title chairman or chairman of the board.

*****

Personal hygiene left much room for improvement. As a result, many women and men had developed acne scars by adulthood. The women would spread beeswax over their facial skin to smooth out their complexions. When they were speaking to each other and a woman began to stare at another woman's face, she was told, "Mind your own beeswax." Should the woman smile, the wax would crack, hence the term "crack a smile." In addition, when they sat too close to the fire, the wax would melt, therefore the expression "losing face."

*****

Ladies wore corsets, which would lace up in the front. A proper and dignified woman, as in "straitlaced," wore a tightly tied lace.

*****

Common entertainment included playing cards. However, there was a tax levied when purchasing playing cards but only applicable to the "ace of spades." To avoid paying the tax, people would purchase 51 cards instead. Yet since most games require 52 cards, these people were thought to be stupid or dumb because they weren't "playing with a full deck."

*****

Early politicians required feedback from the public to determine what the people considered important. Since there were no telephones, TVs, or radios, the politicians sent their assistants to local taverns, pubs, and bars. They were told to go sip some ale and listen to people's conversations and political concerns. Many assistants were dispatched at different times. "You go sip here" and "You go sip there." The two words *go* and *sip* were eventually combined when referring to the local opinion, and thus we have the term *gossip*.

*****

At local taverns, pubs, and bars, people drank from pint- and quart-sized containers. A barmaid's job was to keep an eye on the customers and keep the drinks coming. She had to pay close attention and remember who was drinking in pints and who was drinking in quarts, hence the phrase "minding your Ps and Qs."

*****

One more! I bet you didn't know this! In the heyday of sailing ships, all warships and many freighters carried iron cannons. Those cannons fired round iron cannonballs. It was necessary to keep a good supply near the cannon. However, how to prevent them from rolling about the deck? The best storage method devised was a square-based pyramid with one ball on top, resting on four, resting on nine, which rested on sixteen. Thus, a supply of thirty cannonballs could be stacked in a small area right next to the cannon.

There was only one problem: how to prevent the bottom layer from sliding or rolling from under the others. The solution was a metal plate called a "monkey" with sixteen-round indentations. However, if this plate was made of iron, the iron balls would quickly rust to it. The solution to the rusting problem was to make brass monkeys. Few landlubbers realize that brass contracts much more and much faster than iron when chilled. Consequently, when the temperature dropped too far, the brass indentations would shrink so much that the iron cannonballs would come right off the monkey. Thus, it was quite literally, "Cold enough to freeze the balls off a brass monkey." All this time, you thought that was an improper expression, didn't you?

If you don't send this fabulous bit of historic knowledge to any and all your unsuspecting friends, your floppy is going to fall off your hard drive and kill your mouse.

*****

Food is essential to life; therefore, make it good.
—S. Truett Cathy,
founder of Chick-fil-A.

If you don't believe in history, it's bound to repeat itself.

—Marv Levy

Beauty is only a light switch away.
—Perkins Library, Duke University

If life is a waste of time, and time is a waste of life, then let's all get wasted together and have the times of our lives.

—Amanda's Pizza, DC

Fighting for peace is like screwing for virginity.

No matter how good she looks, some other guy is sick and tired of putting up with her stuff.
—Linda's Bar and Grill, Chapel Hill

One man's fantasy is another man's lunch.

For every good-looking woman, there is another man sick of her.

At the feast of ego, everyone leaves hungry.

It's hard to make a comeback, when you haven't been anywhere.

Make love, not war. Hell, do both. GET MARRIED!

—Women's restroom

If voting could really change things, it would be illegal.

—Revolution Books, NY

If pro is the opposite of con, then what is the opposite of progress? Congress!
—Men's restroom, House of
Representatives, DC

Express Lane: Five beers or less.
—Sign over urinals

You're too good for him.
—Sign over mirror in
women's restroom

No wonder you always go home alone.
—Sign over mirror in
the men's restroom

A Woman's Rule of Thumb:
If it has tires or testicles?
You're going to have trouble with it.
—Women's restroom, Dick's
Last resort, Dallas, Texas

*****

Shopping math: A man will pay $20 for a $10 item he needs. A woman will pay $10 for a $20 item she doesn't need.

Longevity: married men live longer than single men do, but married men are a lot more willing to die...

Propensity to change: A woman marries a man expecting he will change, but he doesn't. A man marries a woman expecting that she won't change, and she does.

It is just another day...

For what?

Another mindless quote.

*****

No one said it would be easy,
They just said it would be worth it.

*****

An obituary printed in the *London Times*.

Today we mourn the passing of a beloved old friend, Common Sense, who has been with us for many years. No one knows for sure how old he was, since his birth records were long ago lost in bureaucratic red tape.

He will be remembered as having cultivated such valuable lessons as knowing when to come in out of the rain, why the early bird gets the worm, life isn't always fair, and maybe it was my fault. Common Sense lived by simple, sound financial policies (don't spend more than you can earn) and reliable strategies (adults, not children, are in charge). His health began to deteriorate rapidly when well-intentioned, but overbearing, regulations were set in place.

Reports of a six-year-old boy charged with sexual harassment for kissing a classmate, teenagers suspended from school for using mouthwash after lunch and a teacher fired for reprimanding an unruly student, only worsened his condition. Common Sense lost ground when parents attacked teachers for doing the job they had themselves failed to do in disciplining their unruly children. It declined even further when schools were required to get parental consent to administer sun tan lotion or an aspirin to a pupil, but could not inform parents when a student became pregnant and wanted to have an abortion.

Common Sense lost the will to live as the Ten Commandments became contraband, churches became businesses; and criminals received better treatment than their victims. Common Sense took a beating when you couldn't defend yourself from a burglar in your own home and the burglar could sue you for assault because you protected yourself and your own.

Common Sense finally gave up the will to live after a woman failed to realize that a steaming cup of coffee was hot. She spilled a little in her lap and was promptly awarded a huge settlement.

Common Sense was preceded in death by his parents, Truth and Trust, his wife, Discretion, by his daughter, Responsibility and his son, Reason. He is survived by his four stepbrothers; I Know My Rights, I Want It Now, Someone Else Is to Blame, I'm A Victim. Not many attended his funeral because so few realised he was gone.

If you still remember him, pass this on.

*****

Women need a reason to have sex. Men just need a place.

—Billy Crystal

While in all you're knowing, know yourself first.

A lady bought a screen door at a hardware store. As she was leaving the clerk said, "Do you need a screw for that?" She said, "No, but I'll blow you for that toaster."

—Roger Miller

Golf: swing hard you might hit it!

Golf is like a good walk spoiled.

—Mark Twain

*****

Why are there eighteen holes on a golf course?

Legend has it that golf started in Scotland in the fifteenth century. An eighteen-hole course was built in St Andrews in 1764. There are eighteen holes as there are eighteen shots in a fifth of Scottish whiskey, so you have a shot of whiskey after each hole. So now you will take eighteen shots, one after each hole.

*****

OK, where were we? Oh yes here we are. Always be where you are, I say. And it's always now, and that's about it. The full significance of the moment is being realized now, thank you, let's move on.

—Willie Nelson

When they throw a war and no one shows up, it will serve as a new beginning of peace on earth. Amen.

—Willie Nelson

The only normal people are the ones you really don't know very well.

—Alfred Adler

Is there water on the other side of that island?

The twist or the twirl? *Whatever!*

Robert Redford's favorite word: *possible.* Robert Redford's least favorite word: *Whatever!!!*

—*Inside the Actors Studio* interview (2005)

I believe that sex is the most beautiful, natural, wholesome things that money can buy.

—Tom Clancy

Having sex is like playing bridge. If you don't have a good partner you better have a good hand.

—Woody Allen

Instead of getting married again, I'm going to find a woman I don't like and just give her a house.

—Rod Stewart

My girlfriend always laughs during sex, no matter what she is reading.

—Steve Jobs

People that think they are crazy enough to change the world are usually the ones that do.

—Steve Jobs

Sex at age 90 is like trying to shoot pool with a rope.

—George Burns

Don't cry because it's over, smile because it happened.

—Dr. Seuss

*****

It's better to be decisive than right.

Most used worst word of 2012: *Whatever!!!*

*****

I had all my medication and it's half past ten. I'm just sitting around waiting for something to kick in.

—Willie Nelson, song in progress

*****

You have a clean slate every day you wake up.

You have a chance every single morning to make that change and be the person you want to be.

We all have personal maintenance every day. You just have to decide to do it. Decide today's the day. Say it: this is going to be my day. Do what you need to do, so you can do what you want to do!

*****

The Job Interview

Interviewer: What do you consider to be your greatest weakness?

Applicant: Honesty!

Interviewer: Humm. I really don't really think honesty is a weakness.

Applicant: I really don't give a shit what you think.

*****

The future belongs to those who believe in the beauty of their dreams.

—Eleanor Roosevelt

In life, you will realize there is a role for everyone you meet. Some will test you, some will use you. But the ones who bring out the best in you, they are the rare and amazing people remind you why it's worth it.

—Unknown

*****

Some great words to live by:

1. Life isn't fair, but it's still good.
2. When in doubt, just take the next small step.
3. Life is too short. Enjoy it.
4. Your job won't take care of you when you are sick. Your friends and family will.
5. Pay off your credit cards every month.
6. You don't have to win every argument. Stay true to yourself.
7. Cry with someone. It's more healing than crying alone.
8. It's okay to get angry with God. He can take it.
9. Save for retirement starting with your first paycheck.

10. When it comes to chocolate, resistance is futile.
11. Make peace with your past so it won't screw up the present.
12. It's okay to let your children see you cry.
13. Don't compare your life to others. You have no idea what their journey is all about.
14. If a relationship has to be a secret, you shouldn't be in it.
15. Everything can change in the blink of an eye, but don't worry, God never blinks.
16. Take a deep breath. It calms the mind.
17. Get rid of anything that isn't useful. Clutter weighs you down in many ways.
18. *Whatever* doesn't kill you really does make you stronger.
19. It's never too late to be happy. But it's all up to you and no one else.
20. When it comes to going after what you love in life, don't take no for an answer.
21. Burn the candles, use the nice sheets, wear the fancy lingerie. Don't save it for a special occasion. Today is special.
22. Overprepare, then go with the flow.
23. Be eccentric now. Don't wait for old age to wear purple.
24. No one is in charge of your happiness but you.
25. Frame every so-called disaster with these words: "In five years, will this matter?"
26. Always choose life.
27. Forgive.
28. What other people think of you is none of your business.
29. Time heals almost everything. Give time, time.
30. However good or bad a situation is, it will change.
31. Don't take yourself so seriously. No one else does.
32. Believe in miracles.
33. God loves you because of who God is, not because of anything you did or didn't do.
34. Don't audit life. Show up and make the most of it now.
35. Growing old beats the alternative of dying young.
36. Your children get only one childhood.

37. All that truly matters in the end is that you loved.
38. Get outside every day. Miracles are waiting everywhere.
39. If we all threw our problems in a pile and saw everyone else's, we'd grab ours back.
40. Envy is a waste of time. Accept what you already have, not what you need.
41. The best is yet to come.
42. No matter how you feel, get up, dress up, and show up.
43. Yield.
44. Life isn't tied with a bow, but it's still a gift.

*****

Family is the most important thing in the world.
—Princess Diana

The world is but a canvas to our imagination.
—Henry David Thoreau

Each person must love their lives as a model for others.
—Rosa Parks

I discovered the secret of the sea in meditation upon a dewdrop.
—Kahlil Gibran

The greatest weakness is giving up. The most certain way to success is to try one more time.
—Thomas Edison

By doing something radically different, I was able
to jump higher than anyone.
                    —Dick Fosbury, inventor of the
                            modern-day high jump

*****

It was the accepted practice in Babylon four thousand years ago that
for a month after the wedding, the bride's father would supply his
son-in-law with all the mead he could drink. Mead is a honey beer,
and because their calendar was lunar based, this period was called the
honey month, which we know today as the honeymoon.

*****

In English pubs, ale is ordered by pints and quarts, so in old England,
when customers got unruly, the bartender would yell at them, "Mind
your pints and quarts, and settle down!" It's where we get the phrase
"mind your Ps and Qs."

*****

Each king in a deck of playing cards represents a great king from history. The king of spades represents King David, hearts, Charlemagne,
clubs, Alexander the Great, diamonds, Julius Caesar.

*****

If a statue in the park is of a person on a horse, which has both front
legs up in the air, the person died in battle. If the horse has one front
leg in the air, the person died because of wounds received in battle. If
the horse has all four legs on the ground, the person died of natural
causes.

*****

Only two people signed the Declaration of Independence on July 4th: John Hancock and Charles Thomson. Most of the rest signed on August 2, but the last signature wasn't added until five years later.

*****

Men can read smaller print then women, but women can hear better.

*****

Coca-Cola was originally green.

*****

Be true to your teeth so they won't be false to you!

*****

> You can't control your circumstances, but you can control what you do with your circumstances.
> —Condoleezza Rice

> Kindness melts defenses. Kindness softens edges. Kindness pierces armor. Kindness eradicates shame. Kindness lightens loads. Kindness awakens hope. Kindness clears debris. Kindness invites connection. Kindness opens hearts. Kindness bridges souls. Kindness inspires kindness. Let us always be kind.
> —Jeff Brown

*****

Wilfred Peterson's phrase, to speak to each other as we face the adventure of a New Year, is "Happy New You." So, my resolutions are: be myself, love myself and let who I am, what I am, what I believe shine. Be the change, love, and peace, I want to see in the world. Be a blessing, be a friend, make a difference. I am what I seek, this means that *Whatever* joy I hope to get, is already in me. All I have to do is make myself available, to what is already inside me. I hope you can join me!!! Happy New Year!

*****

I read about the evils of drinking. I gave up reading.

—Henny Youngman

A mother's love for her child is like nothing else in the world. It knows no law and no pity. It dares all things and crushes down remorselessly all that stands in its path.

—Agatha Christy

Family. We may not have it all together, but together we have it all.

—Robin Roberts

Happiness is the best revenge, because nothing will drive your nemesis crazier than seeing you having a good life and smiling all the time.

I feel sorry for people that don't drink. When they wake up in the morning, that's as good as they're going to feel all day.

—Frank Sinatra

You never hear anyone on their death bed say "Geez, I should have spent more time at the office."

GETTING
LOST
is never a
WASTE
OF TIME

*****

I'm not letting you go, I am accepting you're gone. "Everyone wants happiness, no one wants pain. but you can't have a rainbow, without the rain." As a parent, your own mental happiness is in direct proportion to your least happy child.

WHATEVER

Before you diagnose yourself with depression or low self-esteem, first make sure you're not just surrounded by assholes.

*****

If you obey all the rules, you will miss all the fun.
—Katharine Hepburn

It doesn't take any talent to play hard!
—Derek Jeter

Start where you are, use what you have, do what you can.
—Arthur Ashe

The purpose of life is to be useful, to be honorable, to be compassionate, and to make some difference that you have lived and lived well.
—Ralph Waldo Emerson

*****

The grass is not always greener on the other side. It is greener where you have watered and nurtured it.

*****

If my left thigh is Christmas and my right thigh is New Year's, I hope to see you between the holidays!

*****

There are no losers. Everybody just can't win. "Second place is the first loser." I dislike that saying. You don't have to win you just need to make sure you play!

Remember, it's not who you know, it's who knows you!!!

*****

If a frog had wings it wouldn't bump their behind every time they jump.

—Unknown

Relationships are just like glass. At times it is better to leave it broken than it is to try and hurt yourself putting things back together.

—Unknown

Whatever you give a woman she is going to multiply. If you give her some sperm, she will give you a baby. If you give her a house, she will give you a home. If you give her food, she will give you a meal. If you give her your smile, she will give you her heart. She will multiply all that you give to her. So, if you give her a lot of crap, you will receive a lot of shit.

—William Golding

*****

Letting Go
—Anonymous

To "let go" does not mean to stop caring, it means I can't do it for someone else.

To "let go" is not to cut myself off, it is the realization that I can't control another.

To "let go" is not to enable, but to allow learning from natural consequences.

To "let go" is to admit powerlessness, which means the outcome is not in my hands.

To "let go" is not to change or blame another, it is to make the most of myself.

To "let go" is not to care for, but to care about.

To "let go" is not to fix, but to be supportive.

To "let go" is not to judge, but to allow another to be a human being.

To "let go" is not to be in the middle arranging all the out-comes, but to allow others to affect their destinies.

To "let go" is not to be protective, it permits others to face reality.

To "let go" is not to deny, but to accept.

To "let go" is not to nag, scold, argue, but instead to search out your own shortcomings and correct them.

To "let go" is not to adjust everything to my desires, but to take each day as it comes and cherish myself in it.

To "let go" is not to criticize and regulate anybody, but to try to become what I dream I can be.

To "let go" is not to regret the past, but to grow and live for the future.

To "let go" is to be fear less and love more.

*****

RESENTMENT

The moment you start to resent a person, you become their slave. He controls your dreams, absorbs your digestion, robs you of your peace of mind and goodwill, and takes away the pleasure of your work. He ruins your religion and nullifies your prayers. You cannot take a vacation

without his going along! He destroys your freedom of mind and hounds you wherever you go.
There is no way to escape the person you resent.
He is with you when you are awake. He invades
your privacy when you sleep. He invades your
privacy when you are awake. He is close behind
you when you eat, when you drive your car, and
when you are on the job. You can never have effi-
ciency of happiness. He influences even the tone
of your voice. He requires you to take medication
for the indigestion, headaches, and loss of energy.
He even steels your last moment of consciousness
before you go to sleep. So if you want to be a
slave, harbor your resentments!

—Mark Sichel

*****

Easter egg hunts: proof your child can find things if they want to.

*****

A physician once said, "The best medicine for humans is love."
Someone asked, "What if it doesn't work?"
He smiled and said, "Increase the dose."

*****

Don't walk behind me, I may not lead. Don't
walk in front of me, I may not follow. Just walk
beside me, and help me carry the cooler.

—Unknown.

Quote of the day:
We're not here to have sexual or romantic relationships with them.

> —A Harvard professor on teacher-student relationships, which apparently needed clarification before yesterday.

If you can start the day without caffeine.
If you can always be cheerful, ignoring aches and pains.
If you can resist complaining and boring people with your troubles.
If you can eat the same food every day and be grateful for it.
If you can understand when your loved ones are too busy to give you any time,
If you can take criticism and blame without resentment.
If you can conquer tension without medical help.
If you can relax without alcohol.
If you can sleep without the aid of drugs.
Then you are probably the family dog!

The secret of life: handle every stressful situation like a dog. If you can't eat it or play with it, pee on it and walk away.

> —Unknown

Here I sit brokenhearted, I came to shit and only farted!

> —Unknown

*****

Hearing people chew, makes me want to punch them in the face!

*****

Honk if you love Jesus. Text if you want to meet him.

*****

Easter and April Fools' on the same day. Tell the kids to look for the eggs you didn't hide.

A funny thing to do for the holidays is to take one of your kids' toys and wrap it and then give it to them like a new present. You will have some laughs!

*****

Be happy in front of people you don't like. *It kills them*!

*****

"Always be yourself. Never try to hide who you are. The only shame is to have shame. Always stand up for what you believe in. Always question what other people tell you. Never regret the past, it's a waste of time. There's a reason for everything—every mistake, every moment of weakness, every terrible thing that has happened to you. Grow from it.

The only way you can ever get the respect of others is when you show you show respect for yourself and for them. And most importantly, do your thing and never apologize for being you!" Thank you, Pedro.

The day is what you make it. So why not make it a great one!!
—Steve Schulte

When I stand before God at the end of my life, I would hope that I did not have a single bit of talent left, and I could say, "I used everything you gave me."
—Erma Bombeck

*****

Life is not a race but a journey. Be honest. Work hard. Be choosy. Say "please" and "thank you" and "I love you." Tell someone every day they did a great job. Be thankful for what you have, and don't dwell on what you don't have. You will feel better!

*****

It is always better to keep shooting.

It is better to throw a spear at the moon. You may hit an eagle. If you throw a spear at the eagle, you may only hit a rock. If it were easy, everyone would do it!

*****

Great leaders are almost always great simplifiers, who can cut through argument, debate and doubt, to offer a solution everyone can understand.
—Colin Powell

"I fully believe that there are times that change comes when you least expect it but gives you the opportunity to look at the future differently." (Thanks, Adele P.)

Change is the one thing you can always count on!

If a nice day is predicted for Monday, couldn't there be an executive order to open the liquor stores on Sunday, so North Texas may fully prepare!
—KG Whiskey

Never underestimate the importance of having fun!
—Randy Pausch

Painful truth is better than a pleasant life.
—Bryant McGill

*****

The Skimm.

What to say to your friend who's is always talking about how pot should be legal?

Add this to your list of reasons: A new study compared all kinds of substances and found that pot is one hundred times safer than alcohol. And sometimes comes with brownies. Researchers judged the riskiness of how people typically use drugs like alcohol, heroin, cocaine, etc. They found that booze is actually the deadliest substance of all. The researchers say their findings show that the US law enforcement should focus a lot less on pot-related crimes. So put that in your pipe and smoke it.

Kudos to Colorado, Washington, California, and Alaska. Looks like several others are soon to follow, and they have.

Maybe instead of bombs and bullets being dropped on all the terrorists, we should be dropping bales of weed. Some people just don't understand and others have been ahead of the curve for a long time.

As a song once said, "He's an old hippie, and he don't know what to do / Should he hang on to the old / Should he grab on to the new?"

*****

Whatever you do, you have to do what works for you. Just don't hurt anyone but instead help someone out. Remember everyone doesn't think the same. Everything you learned you learned in kindergarten. Do something nice for someone! Pay it forward!

*****

I need to find a ten-year-old so they can teach me how to use all the stuff on my cell phone.

*****

Today is the first day of the rest of your life! Have you heard that before?

*****

Fantasy football owners

HAPPINESS IS

Yoga, Yoga, and more Yoga

*****

The hardest arithmetic to master is that which enables us to count our blessings.

—Eric Hoffer

Excuses are the nails used to build a house of failure.

—Don Wilder

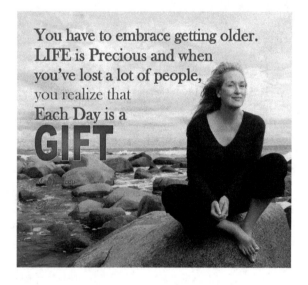

You have to embrace getting older. LIFE is Precious and when you've lost a lot of people, you realize that Each Day is a GIFT

I can choose to let regrets define me, confine me, or refine me, and outshine me. Or I can choose to move on and leave them behind me.

—Unknown

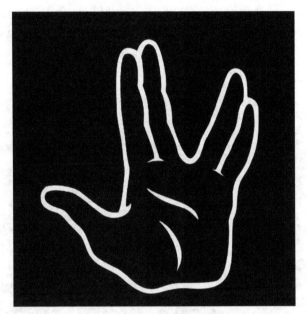

Live long and prosper!

My folks came to the US as immigrants, aliens, and became citizens. I was born in Boston, a citizen, went to Hollywood and became an alien.

—Leonard Nimoy

Life's journey is not to arrive at the grave safely in a well-preserved body, but rather to skid in sideways, totally worn out, shouting holy shit…what a ride!

—Unknown

If you cannot be positive then at least be quiet.
—Joel Osteen

*****

Have you ever just stopped and realized that if you hadn't met a certain person in your life, your life would be completely different?

*****

What is SWAG?
Shit We Ain't Getting

*****

Life is full of maintenance every day.
—Jim Morris (RIP)

You make a living by what you have, but you make a life by what you give.
—Winston Churchill

If you do something easy, life will be hard. If you do something hard, life will be easy.

—Les Brown

You are always one choice away from changing your life.

—Marcy Blochowiak

At the end of the day, it's not happiness that makes us thankful, but thankfulness that makes us happy.

We first make our habits and then our habits make us.

—John Dryden

Serve others and grow rich!

He who has health has hope. And he who has hope has everything.

—Arabian proverb

The key to a successful life is using the good thoughts of wise people.

—Leo Tolstoy

Most people are about as happy as they make up their minds to be.

—Abraham Lincoln

Expect the unexpected! You know it is going to happen, you just don't know what it is. So prepare for it and know that it will happen, and then address it and deal with it.

When we listen, really listen deeply, something shifts during communication.

—Steve Shapiro

The difference in winning or losing is most often…not quitting.

Laughing is an instant vacation.

—Milton Berle

Laughter is also the universal language the same as a smile. You know when you smile at someone, they will smile back. Laugh and you will enjoy it probably as much as the other person. Make it fun and enjoy. Be happy and make them happy.

Laugh loud, and laugh often. It'll keep you happy, keep you healthy, and keep your attitude headed in a positive direction.

—Mac Anderson

A sense of humor is part of the art of leadership, of getting along with people, of getting things done.

—Dwight D. Eisenhower

The most important thing about goals is having one.

—Geoffrey Albert

If I really want to improve my situation, I can work on the one thing over which I have control—myself.

—Stephen R. Covey

Courage is the finest of human qualities because it is the quality which guarantees all the others.

—Winston Churchill

People often tell me, "You know, Zig, motivation doesn't last," and I say… "Bathing doesn't either, that's why I recommend it daily."

—Zig Ziglar

Problems are only opportunities in work clothes.

—Kaiser Permanente

You can't hit a target you can't see.

—Brian Tracy

Feedback is the breakfast of champions.

—Rich Tate

Failure is only the opportunity to begin again more intelligently.

—Henry Ford

You become what you think about.
—Earl Nightingale

Manage stress before it manages you.
—M. Anderson

*****

In the race to be better and best, we forget to just be.

You don't always have to win. But you need to play. Remember, if you win then someone else loses, and that is not good for them. Yes, we all want to win and try to be the best, but you need to at least participate. If you come in second, that is okay. At least you played. Many people will disagree with this and say things like second place is the first loser.

No, it is not. It just means someone else beat you, and it is good for them, and at least you played. Be happy for them.

*****

Enjoy the little things, for one day you may look back and realize they were the big things.
—Robert Brault

Cooperation is the through conviction that nobody can get there unless everybody gets there.
—Virginia Burden

If we did all the things we are capable of, we would literally astound ourselves.
—Thomas Edison

Who say it: Those cannot be done should not interrupt the person doing it!
—Chinese Proverb

Almost all employees, if they see that they will be listened to and they have adequate information they will be able to find ways to improve their own performance and performance of their small work group.
—James O'Toole

*****

When directing and managing people, it is important that you make "we" decisions. Yes, you are in charge, but look at the person who will have to do the work. If you involve them in the decision-making process, they will then become a part of the decision and, in turn, a part of the final outcome. They will take more pride in their work because it was their decision on how to do the task. Don't be an "I guy" or a "my way" type of person. Listen to others and hear their suggestions. Don't let your ego get in the way. Yes, you may have the final decision, but you need them to help you get there.

This can also apply to parenting and raising kids. I don't think there is any reason to explain this. Just do it!

*****

If you take a close look at the most successful people in life, you'll find that their strength is not in having the right answers, but in asking the right questions."
—John Chancellor

*****

You know that no question is stupid, just the question that isn't asked. Also, at times, don't forget to "ask the next questions" i.e., "When will you get here?" Ten minutes.

The next question should be "Where are you now?" Their perception and yours may be a little different. Don't be afraid to clarify.

*****

Great discoveries and achievements invariably involve the cooperation of many minds.
—Alexander Graham Bell

To live is not to learn but to apply.
—Legouve

If a person gets his attitude toward money straight, it will help straighten out almost every other area of his life.
—Billy Graham

A candle loses nothing of its light in lighting another.
—Kahlil Gibran

Each problem that I solved became a rule which served afterwards to solve other problems.
—Rene Descartes

Team members have to be focused on the collective good of the team. Too often, they focus their attention on their department, their budget, their career aspirations, their egos.
—Patrick Lencioni

The greatest discovery of my generation is that human beings can alter their lives by altering the attitudes of mind.

—William James

Passion is the heartfelt energy that flows through us, not from us.

—John Murphy

What lies behind us and what lies ahead of us are tiny matters compared to what lies within us.

—Henry David Thoreau

A man's mind stretched to a new idea never goes back to its original dimensions.

—Oliver Wendell Holmes

Our greatest glory is not in never failing, but in rising up every time we fail.

—Ralph Waldo Emerson

Life is change. Growth is optional. Choose wisely.

—Karen Keiser Clark

Sometimes one single choice not only changes the direction of our lives, but that of many, many others.

—Mac Anderson

Nobody ever did, or ever will, escape from the consequences of his choices.

—Alfred A. Montapert

*****

Remember life is full of maintenance every day! Get err done!

*****

It is one of the most beautiful compensations of life. That no man can sincerely try to help another, without helping himself.
—Ralph Waldo Emerson

We are what we repeatedly do. Excellence then, is not an act, but a habit.
—Aristotle

Whether you think you can, or you think you can't, you're right.
—Henry Ford

Many of life's failures are people who did not realize how close they were to success when they gave up.
—Thomas Edison

Discipline is the bridge between goals and accomplishments.
—Jim Rohn

Take a risk, let yourself love someone else.
—Melody Beattie

Wait a minute, some people may not agree with this.

*****

Remember there are no mistakes, only lessons. Love yourself, trust your choices, and everything is possible.
—Cherie Carter Scott

When it snows, you have two choices: shovel it or make snow angels.

Leadership is action, not position.
—Donald H. McGannon

*****

It is better to be respected as a person first and the position second. Too often we have respect for people because of their position and not because we respect them as a person. Remember we are all just people helping people!

It is better to become a man of virtue than a man of success.

As you climb the ladder of success, you will find when you get to the top that there is nowhere to sit down. How can you climb the ladder to success with your hands in your pockets?

*****

Happiness is not by chance, but by choice.
—Jim Rohn

Attitudes are contagious. Are yours worth catching?
—Anonymous

> A happy person is not a person in a certain set of circumstances, but rather a person with a certain set of attitudes.
>
> —Hugh Downs

> The last of the human freedoms is to choose one's attitude in any given set of circumstances.
>
> —Victor E. Frankl

*****

Success is measured and thought of in many ways: money, jobs, family, friends, contributions, percentages, etc. Each of us have our own reality or perception on what success is. *Whatever* that may be, enjoy it and make what works for you. Remember, everyone doesn't think the same. Just don't hurt anyone and do something nice for someone and don't always think of yourself and your successes but also theirs.

Remember, what is funny for some is not funny for all!

> Success in business as well as in life, is directly dependent on the quality of people you surround yourself with.
>
> —Phil Hickey

How many times did you hear your mom or dad say that to you? "Get some new friends." No, it is not that easy to just get new friends. Negativity breads negativity, but also being positive breads positive thoughts and actions.

Drunks usually hang around other drunks, druggies hang around other druggies, so pick the position you want to be in or the one you think you want to be in, and make it happen. Remember to help yourself and someone else!

*****

I cannot give you a sure-fire formula for success, but I can give you the formula for failure: try to please everybody all the time.
> —Herbert Bayard Swope

You never will be the person you can be, if pressure, tension and discipline are taken out of your life.
> —Herbert Bayard Swope

Have I told you lately that *I Love You?*
> —Van Morrison

The important thing is this: to be able at any moment to sacrifice what we are for what we become.
> —Charles DuBois

Enthusiasm will take you further then talent, title or skill.
> —Robin Crow

It is easy to dodge our responsibilities, but we cannot dodge the consequences of dodging our responsibilities.
> —Sir Josiah Stamp

Humility leads to strength and not to weakness. It is the highest form of self-respect to admit mistakes and to make amends for them.
> —John J. McCloy

All our dreams can come true if we have the courage to pursue them.
> —Walt Disney

It is the nature of man to rise to the greatness if greatness is expected of him.

—John Steinbeck

Always bear in mind, that your own resolution to succeed, is more important than any other one thing.

—Abraham Lincoln

Worry about being better, bigger will take care of itself.

—Gary Comer

*****

Two roads diverged in a wood, and I—
I took the one less traveled by,
And that has made all the difference.

—Robert Frost

*****

It's never too late to be what you might have been.

—George Eliot

*****

What women want: to be loved, to be listened to, to be desired, to be respected, to be needed, to be trusted, and sometimes, just to be held. What men want: tickets for the World Series.

*****

Overtime at times, is a product of mismanagement!

*****

What is your favorite place to go? It is the next place I go to.

*****

The entrepreneur always searches for change, *responds to it*, and exploits it as an opportunity.

*****

He has many of the elements of the hero. His stay with us has given image and a name to the dire entity of slavery, and was an impressive lesson to my children, bringing before them the wrongs of the black man and his tales of woes.
　　—Journal entry of Bronson Alcott (1847)

*****

Nothing can be affected by one man… We must first succeed alone, that we may enjoy our success together.
　　　　　　　　　　　　—Unknown

In the manner of reforming the world, we have little faith in corporations.
　　　　　　　　　　　　—Unknown

Do we call this the land of the free? What is to be free from King George IV and continue the slaves of prejudice? What is to be born free and equal

and not to live? What is the value of any political freedom, but as a means to moral freedom?
—Henry David Thoreau
in his journal (1851)

It's not what you know. It's what you are able to find out in time.
—Kathy R.

I am lost. I've gone to look for myself. If I should return before I get back, please ask me to wait.

Some days you just need to create your own sunshine.

Things work out best, for those who make the best out of how things work out.

Please remove your shoes. And don't take another pair when you leave.

Love is patient; love is kind, it is not angry, proud or rude. Love hopes endures and believes all things. Love never fails.

*****

Perception is reality?

How many times have you heard that? No, perception is not always reality. It is reality of what you saw but not the message being conveyed or that's meant to be conveyed. Don't get caught up in only believing what you see until you get the whole truth and have seen all the facts.

*****

Men to the left

⬅️

➡️

Because women are always right

*****

God didn't promise days without pain, laughter without sorrow, or sun without rain. But God did promise strength for the day, comfort for the tears, and light for the way.

—Anonymous

I'd rather be in a boat, with a drink on the rocks than in the drink, with a boat on the rocks.

—Anonymous

Don't worry about what I'm doing. Worry about why you're worried about what I am doing.

—Anonymous

A recent study has found out that women who carry a little extra weight live longer than men who mention it.

—Anonymous

Great leaders almost always are great simplifiers, who can cut through argument, debate and doubt, to offer a solution everybody can understand.

—Colin Powell

If you are attacked by a mob of clowns, go for the juggler!

There are two things you can do with your head down:
1. Golf
2. Pray

—Lee Trevino

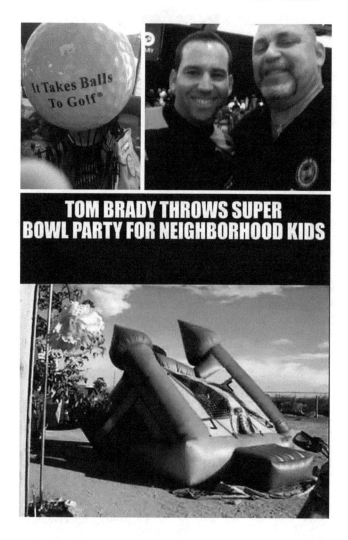

Patriots Super Bowl rings are in.

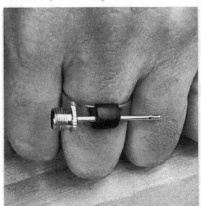

*****

Some of Yogi Berra's words of wisdom:

> "He hits from both sides of the plate. He's amphibious."

> "Baseball is ninety percent mental, and the other half is physical."

> "You better cut the pizza in four pieces, because I'm not hungry enough to eat six."

> Wife asks, "Where would you like to be buried?" "Surprise me."

> "It gets late early out there."

> "I usually take a two-hour nap from 1–4."

> "I think little league is wonderful. It keeps the kids out of the house."

"Why buy good luggage? You only use it when you travel."

"Nobody goes there any more, it's too crowded."

"When you come to a fork in the road take it."

"It ain't over till it's over."

"The future ain't what it used to be."

*****

"I think feeling guilty is a really, really awesome reminder of how much we care about our kids."

You can't worry about it until you know for sure.
—JLS

If you're going to worry about it, you ought to go do it.
—JLS

Resentment embodies a basic choice to refuse to forgive, and unwillingness to let bygones be bygones and bury the hatchet.
—Mark Sichel

In the end, people will judge you anyway. So don't live your life impressing others. Live your life impressing yourself.
—Eunice Camacho Infante

*****

One hundred eighty-six billion e-mails sent and received daily. Over fifty thousand apps downloaded each minute.

Over fifty thousand Uber drivers added globally each month. Somewhere about seven hundred thousand rides a day. I want to know who is counting this stuff?

*****

We shouldn't drop to our knees at any point.
　　　　　　　　　　—Serena Williams

When I walked off the eighteen green I used to cry because there's no more golf. Now I cry when I walk off the ninth hole, because I have to play nine more.
　　　　　　　　　—Dr. Bob Rotella

Awakening to your true nature is like a gentle hurricane. You have no idea where it started or how it found you. You just wake up one day in the burning heart of paradox, and realize you are not a mere guardian or administrator of your life, but your own Co-Founder, CEO and Chief Executive Creator. Nobody, nothing owns you anymore.
　　　　　　　　　　　—Andrea Balt

*****

Live beneath your means.
Return everything you borrow.
Stop blaming other people.
Admit it when you make a mistake.
Give clothes not worn to charity.
Do something nice and try not to get caught.

Listen more, talk less.
Every day take a thirty-minute walk.
Strive for excellence, not perfection.
Be on time.
Don't make excuses.
Don't argue.
Get organized.
Be kind to people.
Be kind to unkind people.
Let someone cut ahead of you in line.
Take time to be alone.
Cultivate good manners.
Be humble.
Realize and accept life isn't fair.
Know when to keep your mouth shut.
Go an entire day without criticizing anyone.
Learn from the past.
Plan for the future.
Live in the present.
Drink water.
Eat properly.
Don't drink and drive.
Don't hurt anyone.
Smile and laugh all the time.
Love thy neighbor as you would love yourself.
Get rid of *all* prejudices.
Don't sweat the small stuff. It's all small stuff!
And don't forget to tip your bartender and server.
Well, that about sums it up!

*****

> Drink the good wine because tomorrow you may
> be dead.
>> —Glenn Frey, at an Eagles sound check

Everything that has ever happened in your life
is preparing you for the moment that is yet to
come.

—Unknown

*****

You know when you are getting older when you barely do anything
all day but you still need to take a nap to continue to do barely
anything.

McDonald's needs a Happy Meal for moms: a bottle of wine,
three Xanax, and a sleeve of Thin Mints.

*****

Surround yourself with people who smile more! Remember that misery loves company. Positive people hang around with positive people.
Negative people gravitate to negative people. Druggies hang around
druggies. They will bring you down and drag you into their world.
You need new friends. Drinkers like to hang around other people
who drink. Sometimes it's not a bad thing but be careful. Drink
wisely. You have the right to choose!

*****

Be honest with yourself. Take responsibility for
yourself.

—Greg Harden, University of
Michigan assistant director

I see myself living in a wonderful place. It fulfills
all my needs and desires. It is a beautiful location
and at a price I can afford.

—Stacy (Thank you.)

The fact that there is a highway to hell, and only a stairway to heaven, says a lot about the antici- pated traffic numbers.

*****

By the time your child is five years old, they will be on the internet at least 570 times, if not more.

Be careful what you post. Only post things that you would want to see on the front-page news.

If a woman says "first of all" during an argument, run away because she has prepared research, data, charts, and possibly a PowerPoint presentation and will destroy you.

How about if you come cut my grass and I'll go mow your lawn and then our neighbors will think we are rich and we can afford a gardener?

I sometimes look back on my life and all I have been through, and I am very thankful that I'm still alive. Smile and be happy!

*****

The difference between the possible and impossi- ble, lies in a person's determination.
—Tommy Lasorda

*****

An Irish Blessing:

May the sun shine, all day long.
Everything go right, and nothing wrong.
May those you love bring love back to you,
And may all the wishes you wish come true.

When Irish eyes are smiling, they are up to something.

*****

Top five most stressful jobs:

1. Enlisted military personnel
2. Firefighter
3. Airline pilot.
4. Police officer
5. Event coordinator
   (Source: Career Cast 2016 Job Stress Report)

Seventy-five percent of workers who voluntarily left their job did so because of their bosses and not the position itself. People don't quit jobs, they quit bosses.

Bosses are like a dirty diaper, always on your ass and full of shit.

*****

Lucky. Get lucky. I wish I were lucky. I need some luck. Why is he so lucky? What about me? They got lucky. I'm so unlucky. I never have any luck.

People say he just got lucky. What is luck?

Luck is when preparedness meets opportunity.

The opportunity was there and you recognized it and took advantage of it so you got lucky.

*****

May love and laughter light you're days, and warm your heart at home. Happy day every day.

*****

Make your friends your do unto another friend.

*****

Question: How did Yale out rebound Baylor?

Answer: "You go up and grab the ball off the rim. When it comes off, you grab it with two hands. You come down with it and that is considered a rebound."

—Taurean Prince

*****

"The only things you can take with you when you leave this world, are things you've packed inside your heart."

—Susan Gale

*****

Now is the time for all good men to come to the aid of their masters. Okay, what does that mean? Oh an old keyboard-typing exercise.

Be thankful and count your blessings for what you have rather than what you want.

*****

It is scary to think that one day we're going to have to live without our mother, father, brother, sister, husband or wife. Or that one day we're were going to have to walk this earth without our best friend by our side or without us. Appreciate your loved ones while you can because none of us are going to be here forever.

—Unknown

You either get bitter or you get better. It's that simple. You either take what has been dealt to you, and allow it to make you a better person, or you allow it to tear you down.

The choice does not belong to fate, it belongs to you!

—Josh Shipp

Stay single until you meet someone who actually compliments your life in a way that makes it better. If not, it's not worth it.

—Unknown

Think not that you can direct the course of love, for love, if it finds you worthy, directs your course.

—Kahlil Gibran

Sometimes I forget to thank the people who make my life happy in so many ways. Sometimes I forget to tell them how much I really appreciate them for being an important part of my life. So, thank all of you, just for being here for me.

—Unknown

When I see lovers, names carved in a tree, I don't think it's cute. I just think it's strange how many people take knives on a date.

—Unknown

*****

Toughness doesn't last, tough people do!

If all good things come to those who wait, is it bad to procrastinate?

*****

> Empty your mind, be formless, shapeless like water. If you put water into a cup it becomes the cup. You put water into a bottle, it becomes the bottle. You put water in a teapot, it becomes the teapot. Now water can flow or it can crash. Be water, my friend.
>
> —Bruce Lee

*****

By the year 2022, there will be 20 billion mobile devices, if not sooner.

*****

> Lead not by an example of your power—but by the power of your example.
>
> —Joe Biden

> The world is but a canvas to our imagination.
>
> —Henry David Thoreau

*****

Here are five reasons why you should think before you speak. The last one is great!

Have you ever spoken and wished that you could immediately take the words back?

Here are the testimonials of a few people who did;

First testimony: "I walked into a hair salon with my husband and three kids in tow and asked loudly, 'How much do you charge for a shampoo and a blow job?' I turned around and walked back out and never went back. My husband didn't say a word. He knew better."

Second testimony: "I was at the golf store, comparing different kinds of golf balls. I was unhappy with the women's type I had been using. After browsing for several minutes, I was approached by one of the good-looking gentlemen who work at the store. He asked if he could help me. Without thinking, I looked at him and said, 'I think I like playing with men's balls.'"

Third testimony: "My sister and I were at the mall and passed by a store that sold a variety of candy and nuts. As we were looking at the display case, the boy behind the counter asked if we needed any help. I replied, 'No, I'm just looking at your nuts.' My sister started to laugh hysterically. The boy grinned, and I turned beet red and walked away. To this day, my sister has never let me forget."

Fourth testimony: "Have you ever asked your child a question too many times? My three-year-old son had a lot of problems with potty training and I was on him constantly. One day, we stopped at Taco Bell for a quick lunch in between errands. It was very busy with a full dining room. While enjoying my taco, I smelled something funny, so of course I checked my seven-month-old daughter and she was clean. Then I realized that Danny had not asked to go potty in a while. I asked him if he needed to go and he said 'No.' I kept thinking, *Oh Lord, that child has had an accident, and I don't have any clothes with me.*

"Then I said, 'Danny, are you *sure* you didn't have an accident?'

"'No,' he replied.

"I just KNEW that he must have had an accident because the smell was getting worse.

"So I asked one more time, 'Danny did you have an accident?'

"This time he jumped up, yanked down his pants, bent over, spread his cheeks and yelled, 'See, Mom? It's just farts!' while thirty people nearly choked to death on their tacos laughing. He calmly pulled up his pants and sat down. An old couple made me feel better, thanking me for the best laugh they'd ever had!"

Last but not least testimony: This had most of the state of Michigan laughing for two days and a very embarrassed female news anchor who will, in the future, likely think before she speaks. What happens when you predict snow but don't get any? We had a female news anchor that, on the day after it was supposed to have snowed and didn't, turned to the weatherman and asked, "So, Bob, where's that eight inches you promised me last night?"

Not only did he have to leave the set, but half the crew did too. They were laughing so hard!

Now didn't that feel good? Remember, we all say things we don't really mean. Think before you speak!

*****

Good friends are like stars. You don't always see them, but you know they are always there.

Life isn't about finding yourself. Life is about creating yourself.
—George Bernard Shaw

When you mail things, you sometimes don't know if it got there. You just know if it didn't.

Turn your face to the sun and let the shadows fall behind you.
—Vincent Jermaine

*****

George asks, "We're going to order Chinese. What do you want?"
Kramer replies, "I don't care. *Whatever.*"

*****

You're not as young as you use to be but not as old as you're going to be.

Winning is the only thing. How often have you heard that? But when you win, it means someone else loses and it is not good for them. Many times, it is more important to play and participate and you don't have to win. Have fun. But also winning is fun. 2nd place is not the first looser. At least they played.

> Work together, problems can become opportuni-
> ties when the right people come together.
> —Robert Redford

How true is this? We all need to work together as we should all have a common goal. I feel a lot of politicians forget this all the time. What about me?

Having the right kinds of friends can make all the difference. Good people usually hang around good people. Bad people usually hang around bad people. Druggies usually hang around druggies. Drunks usually hang around drunks. Gang members with other gang members, gamblers hang around other gamblers. Positive people usually hang around other positive people. The list just goes on and on. You can't just pick your friends, but you have to be sure that the people you call your friends are really your friends and not just taking you down their wrong paths. Misery loves company. How true at times can this statement be?

*****

Once you let your grief become anger, it will never go away.

—Lost

*****

Dwyane Wade comment, "They have a statue of Rocky and he's not even real."

Charles Barkley replies, "*Whatever!*"

*****

If God's not a Bronco fan, then why are the sunsets orange? Yeah, *Whatever.*

*****

"'Why are they going to watch it?'
''Cause it's on TV…'"

—Seinfeld

"'Why are they going to read it?'
''Cause it's *Whatever!*'"

*****

I turned my monitor upside down and saw your team is in 1ˢᵗ place.

*****

Elaine asks, "How do you know it shrinks?"

George replies, "I don't know. It just does."

Elaine says, "I don't know how you guys walk around with those things. If I had one of those, I would never come out of the house."

But I don't want to be a pirate.

—Seinfeld

*****

You will never lose money, if you always take a profit.

Minds are like parachutes. They only function when open.

—Thomas Dewar

'Cause you were just too busy being fabulous, too busy to think about us.

—Eagles

*****

When you just can't believe what you just heard or why someone would do or say something you don't agree with, remember everyone just doesn't think the same. This may not be right, but it's just the way it is.

You can learn so much of what not to do from other people.

You are what you eat. Okay, what does that mean?

*****

The grass is not always greener on the other side.

—James Taylor

Sometimes it is better to beg for forgiveness, than to ask for permission.

To give a real service you must add something which cannot be bought or measured with money, and that is sincerity and intensity.

—Douglas Adams

Obstacles are what we see when you take your eyes off the goal.

—Henry Ford (1923)

*****

Well the hay is in the barn, so now let us see if it rains.

*****

As you move forward, you become what you think.

—Gerald O'Dell

Love is a fruit in season at all times and within reach of every hand.

—Mother Theresa

*****

If it were easy, then everyone would do it.
Work smarter not harder.
Be a DWIT. Do What It Takes!
At times you need to secure your own oxygen before helping others. Think about that one. Listen to the flight attendants.
Today is the first day of the rest of your life, so make it the best.

*****

Save my neck here, that's what I do. *Whatever.*
—Erik, *Survivor*

He can do *Whatever* he can do to stay in the game.

—Ami about Erik, *Survivor*

Erik to Ozzy from *Survivor*, "Ami was trying to sway Amanda to do *Whatever*."

*****

Life isn't about waiting for the storm to pass. It's about learning to dance in the rain.

Getting a first kiss it like getting pickles out of a jar. Once you get the first the rest comes easy.

If this house is rocking then just come in without knocking.

*****

Believe and achieve! Don't drive faster than your guardian angel can fly. Some people just need an AA sometimes, an Attitude Adjustment. You should have, do on to other friends.

*****

The longer I'm gone, the stronger I find, you walking around in my mind.

—Jim Morris

The longer you're gone
the stronger I find
you walking around
in my mind!!

RIP Jim, you were one of the unknown best.

*****

PHD. Pile higher and deeper.

BOHICA. Bend Over Here It Comes Again! Sometimes you just need to say BOHICA, and it may make you feel better, as that is the way it is, and you just accept it. Thanks, Dave

*****

Do what you need to do, so you can do what you want to do.

—Denzel Washington

Do what you have to do until you can do, what you want to do.

—Oprah Winfrey

Do what you prepared yourself to do.
—Denzel Washington

*****

Man gives you an award and God gives you a reward.

Tough as a two-dollar steak.

You can lead a horse to water but you can't make him drink. (What does that mean?)

Like pissing in the wind?

All good things come to those who wait! Yeah, but I'm tired of waiting.

If it ain't broke, don't fix it.

Laughter is the universal language. USE IT! And don't forget to smile also. A smile goes a *looooong* way. Turn that frown upside down.

New friends are great but old friends know where you have been. Keep in touch.

At times in life and in business, you need to respect the position and not the person. Even though it is more important to be respected as a person first.

"How is business today?" Wait before we get into the business conversation. Say "Good morning! How are you today?" first. Respect the person first as an individual and the business or position second. We are all people first, so don't forget that!

*****

Be what you want to be.

—Gandhi

It's a relief, when you don't suck.

—Laura Linney

*****

Have good work habits! Remember, do you want *you* working for *you*?

Do you want to be in a foxhole with this person when the going gets tough? They may be great to be around and have fun with, but sometimes things just need to get done.

*****

When the going gets tough the tough gets going.
—Joseph P. Kennedy

With the absence of pressure, it's hard to do great things.

—Geno Auriemma

Definition of management is getting work done through others.

—AMA,
American Management Association

*****

Even with all the scouting, it still comes down to execution.
David Wright, another reason to get to third base. Thanks, Jodi.

It's raining. No, it's clearing up. Yeah, clear up to your ass.

*****

"Are you a member of the tribe?"
"Yes, the nookie tribe."

*****

"He was so fast; he could turn out the lights and
be under the covers before it got dark." Satchel
Paige, baseball pitcher

Relationships start with a single date.

*****

LEADERS

Leaders are made, they are not born, and they are
made just like anything else has ever been made
in this country—by hard effort. And that's the
price that we all have to pay to achieve that goal
or any goal. And despite of what we say about
being born equal, none of us are born equal but
rather unequal. And yet the talented are no more
responsible for their birthright than the under-
privileged. And the measure of each should be
what each does in a specific situation.

It is becoming increasingly difficult to be tol-
erant of a society who has sympathy only for the
misfits, only the maladjusted, only for the criminal,

only for the loser. Have sympathy for them, help them, help them, but I think it's also time for all of us to stand up for and to cheer for the doer, the achiever, one who recognizes a problem and does something about it, one who looks at something extra to do for his country, the winner, the leader!
—Vince Lombardi

When the power of love overcomes the love of power, the world will know peace.
—Indian proverb

Competitive games need competitive men.
—Vince Lombardi

Winner winner chicken dinner.

We eat what we want and sell the rest.
—Blue Bell Creameries

It takes no talent to hustle.
—Matt Millen

We will all end up on a reality TV show. Just do the numbers.
—DJ

"'You asked my wife to be in a three-some?'
'Ex-wife.'
'Whatever.'"
—Larry David, Curb your Enthusiasm

*****

The Meantime

Remember everything is for the meantime. The meantime can be just a short time or a long time or *Whatever*. If you don't like the situation you are in, remember it is only for the meantime. It is not like it's going to last forever. So just deal with it. Make the best of it and carry on. One thing that we can always count on is change. Change is inevitable. It will happen weather we want it or not. Go with it. Change can be good. Yes, change can also be bad. So now it is up to you to change it so it is good for you or someone else. Remember it's only for the meantime. This is really easy to say, but when you begin to learn to accept this, you will see and feel the results.

It is not where you start, it's where you end up. Hopefully we will all end up in the right place.

It's what's up front that counts. That's from an old cigarette ad. I'll leave that to your imagination.

Aren't some situations just the time out of your life you'll never get back?

Remember that your job usually affects someone else's job. Even the little things such as ordering dinner properly or taking out the garbage. If you don't put it out properly, the garbageman cannot pick it up properly. Almost everything we do affects someone else. Keep it positive, and don't always think about yourself. "When did we stop talking about me?" If you don't do your job with an assist, then other person cannot score a point. Carry out your job so it will help another person do their job.

*****

An older woman goes to the pharmacist and asks, "Sir, do you have those little cotton balls?"

"No. What the hell do think I am? A teddy bear?"

*****

An older gentleman goes into the pharmacist and asks, "Sir, can I get half a pill of Viagra?

"Half a pill? That won't do you any good."

"No, I don't need it for sex. I just need it so I can stop pissing on my shoes."

*****

Frank was standing at the urinal. Just then, the door busted open and an Afro American gentleman came running in.

"Whew," he said as he stood at the urinal, "I just made it!"

Frank looked over and said, "Can you make me one in white?"

Thanks, Frank, for all you did for me and the others you touched in your life. RIP.

*****

In baseball they say when you are out, you are out. It's the same way in politics.

—Gerald Ford

Today is the first day of the rest of your life. Hello!

Like my daddy always said, "If you can't get in the front door, just go around the back."

—J. R. Ewing

If you see a snake, kill it. Don't appoint a committee on snakes.

—H. Ross Perot

He who profit most is he who serves best.

—Howard E. Butt

A team that won't be beat, can't be beat.

Aerodynamically the bumblebee shouldn't be able to fly, but the bumblebee doesn't know it. So it goes on flying anyway.

—Mary Kay Ash

You have to do a little bragging on yourself, even to relatives. Man doesn't get anywhere without advertising.

—John Nance Garner.

Consumers are statistics, customers are people.

—Stanly Marcus

Art is a legalized form of insanity, and I do it very well.

—Stanley Marsh 3

See you at the top.

—Zig Ziglar

Become so wrapped up in something, that you forget to be afraid.

—Lady Bird Johnson

If you think that hiring an expert is expensive, wait till you hire an amateur.

—Red Adair

Decide what you want. Decide what you are willing to exchange for it. Establish your priorities and go to work.

—H. L. Hunt

He's all hat and no cattle.

—A Texas saying

A Texan is a Texan wherever he may be.

—Amon Carter

Nowhere but Texas, Lone Star and Longnecks.

He beat him by a dip and a half? NASCAR. No wonder, three more left turns.

*****

Poker, a hard way to make an easy living.

—Mike Sexton

Go low. You can always back into a high poker hand.

A heart is not judged by how much you love but rather how much you are loved by others.

—The Wizard of OZ

As you are going through life you better know what not to poke.

—Kevin Costner

Every game is a championship, so here we go.
>—Pete Carroll

*****

Those who dare to fail miserably can achieve greatness.
>—John F. Kennedy

To give real service you must add something which cannot be bought or measured with money, and that is sincerity and intensity.
>—Douglas Adams

I say we vote for JT anyway because we can all beat him at *Whatever*.
>—*Survivor*

If we have to go to Staples, Kinko's or *Whatever*.
>—Annie Duke, *Apprentice*

"'Say hello to your little sister for me.'
'You don't know my little sister.'
'*Whatever*.'"
>—George

It was BBQ sauce, hot and spicy, *Whatever*.
>—Simon

We are all parents. We talk about the reality of parenting. You don't like it when your kids misbehave or *Whatever*.
>—Meredith Vieira

Regardless of who I am talking to or *Whatever*, the only allegiance I have in this game is Joe.

—Erin, *Survivor*

You can take that money, you know, and put it in a rainy-day fund or *Whatever*.

—Joe Biden

She kept her website. I'll market it through *Whatever*.

—Guy behind me on a plane

*****

When you can, try counting the number of times you hear the word *Whatever* one day. I have done this several times and not telling anyone. There are some days it is up to ten to fifteen times just in conversations. It's really amazing just like some other buzzwords of the past like bitchen, cool, rad, far-out, etc. They seem to appear for a bit and then just fizzle out and then maybe make a comeback…*not*. But *Whatever* is and will always be there!

*****

I could be wrong, *Whatever*, Cleveland's on the clock.

—Announcer

Why don't they make cigarettes out of *Whatever?* That is, if it's harmless, why don't people smoke Styrofoam or *Whatever* you are putting in your mouth.

—Ellen DeGeneres

Can you tear someone a new one who already is one?

—Dennis Miller

*****

Oh, I'm sorry I called you a a———hole. I thought you already knew.

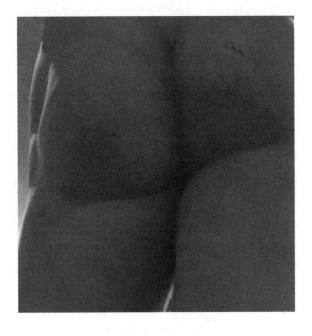

*****

The last game we beat them by *Whatever.*

—Phil Jackson

*****

Accept the changes, run with it. Out of the ashes rose the phoenix. This was change. What we can always count on is change. Change is good. Look at the positive side. Look at what it can a will do for you in the future. If you cannot accept change, then you will be stuck, unable to move on, and if you do, you will be miserable. Make the best out of it. As Bob Dylan once said back in the sixties that still holds true today, "for the times they are a-changin'."

*****

Take Time
Martin Greyford

Take time to think.
It is the source of power.
Take time to play.
It is the secrete of perpetual youth.
Take time to read.
It is the fountain of wisdom.
Take time to pray.
It is the greatest power on Earth.
Take time to be friendly.
It is the road to happiness.
Take time to laugh.
It is the music of the soul.
Take time to give.
It is too short of day to be selfish.
Take time to work.
It is the price of success.
Take time to do charity.
It is the key to heaven.

*****

Time to Pray
Author Unknown

I got up early one morning
and rushed right into the day;
I had so much to accomplish
that I didn't have time to pray.

Problems just tumbled about me
and heavier came each task
"Why doesn't God help me?" I wondered
He answered, "You didn't ask."

I wanted to see joy and beauty,
but the day toiled on grey and bleak;
I wondered why God didn't show me.
He said, "Why you didn't seek?"

I tried to come into God's presence;
I used all my keys at the lock.
God, gently and lovingly chided,
"My child, you didn't knock."

I woke up early in the morning
and paused before entering the day
I had so much to accomplish
That I had to take time to pray.

*****

Recycling today is so important. It is how we will leave this world to our future generations. Unless we all contribute and take baby steps, we will self-destruct ourselves or we will take the easy way out and save it for the next person. Sometimes it is easier to bitch about something than it is to act on. Here also is what you can do. Still a little confusing:

*****

The Man Who Thinks He Can

If you think you are beaten, you are,
If you think that you dare not, you don't,
If you'd like to win, but you think you can't,
It's almost certain you won't."

—Unknown

*****

At the airport, you must first try and find a *USA Today* newspaper prior to buying one. Hopefully someone has recycled one for you. The only exception to this is if you are the first one at the airport. Then you should start the cycle and buy one. It is now your responsibility to leave it for the next person. Drop it on a chair, on top of the recycle bin, or just hand it to someone. DO NOT throw it away. So just read it and leave it. You have done a good deed and also helped someone out even though a newspaper may be a thing of the past. But this opportunity can and will apply to other things. Pay it forward when you can.

*****

I like to think of ideas as potential energy. They're really wonderful, but will do nothing happen until we risk putting them into action.
—Mae Jemison

Adversity doesn't build character. It reveals it.
—Vince Lombardi

Did you hear they are building a new Starbucks down the street? Where? Inside the Starbucks.
—Dennis Miller

Quality of your education directs the quality of your education.
—Joe Morgan

*****

At times, things are said in the heat of battle and things are done in the emotion of the moment. Remember we don't always express ourselves correctly, and at times, we say things we really don't mean and then we apologize for them. Other times, we may need to use it as controlled anger such as you are disciplining a child and you may need to raise your voice to get your point across. Use your controlled anger wisely and do not abuse. Please don't hurt anyone emotionally and or physically!

Remember that life is like a pendulum. It is constantly swinging side to side, getting higher and then going back down and swinging up on the other side. When you are really swinging low, know that the pendulum will eventually go back up. Also, if it is too high, it may start to go back down. You are in charge of your own pendulum. Control it, and make it work for you.

*****

Mechanical engineers build weapons, civil engineers build targets.

—Dr. Mae Jamison, astronaut

Through our greatest adversities come our greatest successes.

—Marcus Aurelius

I'm not talking about cutting me open. I'm talking about giving me blood tests, X-rays or *Whatever.*

—*Unusuals*

You know it is really good to see you, even though you are a hallucination or *Whatever.*

—Unusuals

"'What is this?'
'The Human Fund. *Whatever.*'"

—Seinfeld

I nicked it three of four days ago and it got infected. I wish it wouldn't have happened, but *Whatever...*

—*Survivor*

*****

A Short Course in human relations:

The Six most Important Words:
"I admit I made a mistake."
The Five most Important Words:
"You did a good job."
The Four most Important Words:
"What is your opinion?"
The Three most Important Words:
"If you please."
The Two most Important Words:
"Thank you."
The One most Important Word:
"We"
The Least Important Word:
"I"

—Unknown

*****

Speak Up

Everyone is entitled to make a fool of himself. Remain silent and people will think of you as a fool anyway.

It is more important to become a person of value than a person who is successful.

Be respected for who you are and not the position or title you have!

If you unconsciously live a conscious life, you can never be poor. *What?*

*****

Here we stand, hand in hand, on a threshold of a dream.

—Moody Blues

Why be lonely for something you don't have?

—JLS

*****

WE DECISIONS

It is important at times to make "we" decisions. Everyone usually wants to do it their way. How do you want to slice the bread? It doesn't matter, as we are going to eat it anyway. When you have an idea and you share it, the other person also has an opinion. Hey, don't we all? Yours may be right and theirs may be right also. So if you take a little bit of your idea and take a little of their idea and then you come up with a third idea, this makes you both have ownerships of the task, and a better job will be done to complete the task, as both of you have taken ownership of the task. And you will have more pride in the task instead of just doing it one way because you were told to do it that way. Remember you don't have to win. You just need to play. *We* is a very powerful word. Use it wisely!

*****

Time will tell. As Jimmy Buffett said, "I bought a new watch and the time just says now." Don't you want a watch like that?

*****

"I could see into the eyes of the great fish," George says.

"Mammal," Jerry corrects.

"*Whatever.*" George replies.

Conrad says, "I got to go."
"Stay, go, *Whatever.*" Jerry says.

*****

Word to consumers. Don't spend money you don't have. Always try to live one step below your means and you will feel wealthy. This is not the government talking.

It is true that almost everything we become and accomplish in life is with and through other people. The ability to create rapport with people is the most important skill we can learn.

*****

A gold medal is a wonderful thing, if you're not enough without it, you'll never be enough with it.
—John Candy, *Cool Running*

At what point in time did we become a society that had to have bottled water? Was it April 4, 1992?
—Dennis Miller

Makes you wonder. I guess we can't drink out of the hose anymore?

*****

"How long will this lightbulb last?"
"A lightbulb like that...in a warm, dry climate can last fifty to eighty years."
"Well, how long if I turn it on?"

*****

> The care of human life and happiness, and not
> their destruction, is the first and only object of a
> good government.
> —Thomas Jefferson

*****

Laughter and a smile are the universal languages. Use it!

*****

I sat next to an old man on a plane once.

He said, "All the kids under the age of twenty should be put in a twenty-foot hole until they are older. I have seen the lights of New York and I have seen the lights of Paris. But my favorite lights are the taillights of the car as my grandchildren are leaving."

This seemed to be a real negative person. Cherish your time with them. Some people don't have any. Too bad he will live out his "golden years" with that attitude!

Say it ain't so, Joe! Say it ain't so!

*****

> There are three kinds of people in this world:
> those who make it happen, those who watch
> things happen, and those who stand around and
> say, "What happened?"
> —Tommy Lasorda

*****

Do you know Jack Schitt?

For some time, many of us have wondered just who is Jack Schitt? We are at a loss when someone says, "You don't know Jack Schitt."

Jack Schitt is the only son of Awe Schitt.

Awe Schitt, the fertilizer magnet, married Miss O. Needeep. They had one son, Jack.

In turn, Jack Schitt married Noe Schitt. This deeply religious couple had six children: Hollie Schitt, Giva Schitt, Fulla Schitt, Bull Schitt, and then the twins, Deep Schitt and Dip Schitt.

Against her parent's objections, Deep Schitt married her cousin, Dumb Schitt, a high school dropout.

After being married for fifteen years, Jack and Noe Schitt divorced.

Noe Schitt latter married Ted Sherlock, and because her kids were living with them, she wanted to keep her previous name. She was then known as Noe Schitt Sherlock.

Meanwhile, Dip Schitt married Loda Schitt, and they had a son with a rather nervous disposition named Chick N. Schitt.

Two of the other six children, Fulla Schitt and Giva Schitt, were inseparable throughout childhood and subsequently married the Happen brothers in a dual ceremony. The Schitt-Happens nuptials.

The Schitt-Happens children were Dawg, Byrd, and Horse. Bull Schitt, the prodigal son, left home to tour the world. He recently returned from Italy with his new bride, Pisa Schitt.

Now you know Jack Schitt. Not original but still funny.

*****

I'm so low, I can play handball against the curb.

I'm so broke I can't even afford to pay attention.

*****

In life, paying attention and learning from our peers (or others) is a mark of real maturity.
—Orel Hershiser

*****

Remember, we can learn so much of what not to do or how not to act from others. Take heed to the negative and turn it into your positive. See what the other person is doing right. We all have something to give each other even if it is negative, so we can learn from that.

More organized people are at the top, and that makes a lot of other people's jobs easier.

In work and play, it is important to anticipate the needs of others. Your turn to think about that.

At times, we need to use our active listening skills. Don't be so hung up on thinking only of ourselves. "When did we stop talking about me?" said George. During a conversation, you may be listening to a story or an incident someone is telling you about. It will trigger a thought in your mind about one of your own experiences. All you do now is focus on your thoughts and you are not engaged and listening to their story, as you are so focused on wanting to tell your story. Remember, it is not about you. Your turn will come to tell your story. Pay attention to others. Show some empathy for them.

Never miss an opportunity to shut up.
—Mark Twain

Never try and play video poker and sit down next to a person playing ten-cent Keno video game and winning. The noise will drive you crazy. Especially if they are chain-smoking.

This isn't rocket science. Yes but there is still stuff we need to do.

*****

When you win, nothing hurts.
—Joe Namath

This getting old is not for sissies.
—my mother

*****

The constitution says "we the people." It does not say "we the Democrats, we the Republicans, we the Whigs, we the Tories, we the gays, we the lesbians, we the socialites, we the etc." It says, *we the people*. Remember, we are just people helping people who should be helping others. Why do we forget that so often?

*****

> Though preparation was non-negotiable, but excellence was always the goal. When the job was done well, even if no one noticed but me, it was a reward enough. Rather than trusting my instincts and pushing through my fears, I allowed the negative to overwhelm the possible positive solution. We can all live in isolation or we can make room for these people in our hearts.
> —Orel Hershiser

> If you fail to plan then you plan to fail.
> —Benjamin Franklin

*****

Because the process was more important than the results, self-discipline refused to cut corners or give up.

*****

> Motivation is simple. You eliminate those who are not motivated.
> —Lou Holtz

*****

The flowers are wilted but the memories will last forever.

*****

> Leadership is a potent combination of strategy
> and character. But if you must be without one,
> be without strategy.
> —Norman Schwarzkopf

*****

If you don't have tough days, you don't have good stories. So true in
many of our jobs and our daily lives. In the work place, think that if
there weren't bumps, they wouldn't need you.

Safest job for job security: a copy repairman. You will always
have work.

*****

> Hard work keeps the wrinkles out of the mind
> and spirit.
> —Helena Rubenstein

> Care for your body as if you were going to live
> forever. Care for your soul as if you were going to
> die tomorrow.
> —Unknown

I know we all need to adhere to these words more often!

*****

> Why does a doctor open a practice?
> Because sometimes we feel they are just practicing
> on us and they don't really know.

Dammit, Jim. I am a doctor not a god.

—Bones

*****

We have to judge the work we do and take responsibilities for our actions.

She's so good, she can convince a dog to jump off a meat truck.

*****

He's not Korean, he's Chinese, *Whatever.*
—Fast and Furious

Are you going to mix this in or fold it in or *Whatever?*

—Matt Lauer

*****

Remember: Everybody doesn't think the same.

*****

He closed cases, he got things done, and the rest is just *Whatever.*

—*Unusuals*

All the consumers are looking for convince and you make up this new *Whatever*, and how do we get this message out to the consumers?

—*Apprentice*

I am always the one to step up *Whatever*, wherever.
—*Apprentice*

Do you want a job? A JOB is Just Over Broke

Where you start is not as important as where you finish.

—Zig Ziglar

I'm just preparing my important remarks.

—Winston Churchill

Sometimes good command responses get accompanied by bad emotional decisions.

—*Lost*

We are what we readily do. Excellence then is not an act but a habit.

—Aristotle

What laws have I broken? Is it wrong for me to love my own? Is it wicked for me because my skin is red? Because I am Tatanka Iyotanka; because I was born where my father lived, because I would die for my people and my country.

—Sitting Bull (1877)

Let me be a free man, free to travel, free to stop, free to work, free to trade where I choose, free to choose my own teachers, free to follow religion of my fathers, free to think and talk and act for myself.

—Chief Joseph (1879)

Don't take anything personally. Nothing others do is because of you. What others say and do is a projection of their own reality, their own dream. When you're immune to their opinions and actions of others, you won't be the victim of needless suffering.

—Miguel Ruiz

"Is that you? I think the M&M should be you."
"*Whatever.*"

—Seinfeld

Golf is an easy game, just hard to play. Tee Times: Keep your head down, flex your knees, firm up your grip, watch the ball, don't bend your elbow, step into the ball, don't rush your swing, follow through and RELAX.

No wonder golf is so tough. Who can remember all that?

We golfers do not lose golf balls, we just exchange them.

When you are looking for your ball from an errant shot, you will probably find another ball that someone else lost. Someone will eventually find the ball you lost. So it is a good thing that you gave your ball to someone else and therefore you should not be charged a penalty stroke, as you are giving your ball to someone else, and that is a nice thing to do: to give someone something!!!

A pretty good day on the course!

*****

Golf can best be described as an endless series of tragedies, obscured by the occasional miracle, followed by a good bottle of beer.

When a defining moment comes along, you define the moment…or the moment defines you.
—Kevin Costner, *Tin Cup*

The ability to control thought process is to concentrate on a task. It is almost universally recognized as the most important key to effecting performance in sport.
—Robert M. Nideffer

Art is what you can get away with.
—Andy Warhol

We don't inherit the earth. We borrow it from our children.

Say less so you don't have to take much back.

Accept change, deal with it and know that it is coming.

There is bad change and good change. Change is not a destination, just as hope is not a strategy.
—Rudy Giuliani

*****

Accept the changes. Run with it. Out of the ashes rose the phoenix. This was change. What we can always count on is change. Change is good. Look at the positive side. Look at what it can do for you in the future. If you cannot accept change, then you will be stuck, unable to move on, and if you do, you will be miserable. Make the best out of it. As Bob Dylan once said back in the sixties that still holds true today, "the times, they are a-changin'."

*****

The Unexpected

Just know and realize the unexpected is going to happen. You don't know what it is, but it will happen. Prepare for it. You know that the unexpected will happen and you don't know what it is that is why it is called "the unexpected." When it does come, embrace it, take ownership of it, enjoy it. Learn to deal with the situation at hand and run with it. You can't control the unexpected, but you can control what you do about it and what actions you take.

*****

The harder I work, the luckier I get.
—Thomas Jefferson

We're out of whole wheat. *Whatever!* I'm starving.
—*Heroes*

Whatever, Whatever, Whatever, it's the vocals that matter.
—Randy Jackson

You are responsible for your life.
—Oprah Winfrey

*****

A recent study found that the average American walks about 900 miles a year. Another study found Americans drink on the average of 22 gallons of alcohol a year. That means, on average, Americans get about 41 miles to the gallon.

Makes you proud to be an American, doesn't it!

Hey man, what kind of lite beer do you want? *Whatever*, they all taste the same.
—Miller Lite

*****

Anger is a choice!

*****

A huge *Whatever* is texting. You can't even understand it with all the "LOL," "CU," ":)," "OMG," "LAMO," "BFF," "WTF," "GFY," "FOMO." Oh and not to mention all the emojis, just to name a few. There will be, if not already, a dictionary that will list all of these so we can just communicate in abbreviated languages. Our society will all walk around hunchbacked from leaning over to text and looking at our devices all the time. *Whatever* happened to just picking up the phone and calling someone and talking? Now that's old fashioned, isn't it? Or you can actually handwrite them a letter and then mail it.

If you play the right hands, you will win. Now that's a profound statement.

*****

> The secret of management is to keep the guys who
> hate you away from the guys who are undecided.
> —Casey Stengel

*****

Beware of getting vacationitis. You know you are going on vacation soon and your productivity goes south because you are so focused on your vacation rather than the task at hand. Take care of today, and do what you need get done. Your vacation will come soon, and you will have a better attitude and enjoy your vacation even more, as you will have accomplished what you needed to accomplish before you left.

You've got to control yourself before you can control your horse.

Wind in My Hair
Stephen A. Gregory—American Cowboy

I ride my majestic friends with the wind in my hair.
No greater sense of freedom we haven't a care.
The smell of his sweat as we quicken our pace.
The sun, the rain, or the snow on my face.
Two wild spirits in a bond so peaceful yet rare,
and I always ride with the wind in my hair.

Time in the saddle seems to always fly bye,
like life's best years in the blink of an eye.

So, if I should pass in this majestic way,
on a young colt or on my own Bay,
remember it's my choice, and I had not a care,
and I lived for the feel of the wind in my hair.

As my friends all know and my mother might say,
A spirit like his, had to have his own way.
Try not to be sad, for he rode without fear,
the only place his mind and conscious clear,
no worries or doubt or even a care,
and he always rode with the wind in his hair.

A true cowboy is one who says it was nothing
when it was everything and that believes that he
did better than first but worse than last.

—Cowboy quiz

*****

Courage is being scared to death and saddling up
anyway.

—John Wayne

*****

Adopting the right attitude can convert a negative stress into a positive one.

—Hans Seyle

I've never been poor, only broke. Being poor is a
frame of mind. Being broke is only a temporary
situation.

—Mike Todd

*****

Retail term, a sign is an invitation to buy but not a contract to sell.
How many times have you heard that?

*****

It's important that you and I get along. Do you want me to do it? *Whatever.*

       —Amazing Race

Whatever, Casey, I just don't know how Sarah is going to feel about this.

Try not to stay in screen saver mode: A lot of movement and no productivity.

We are terrorists, like the people who can read minds or *Whatever.*

       —Heroes

Other people might feel trapped or confined or *Whatever.*

     —Oprah about the FLDS

I know it's not protocol or *Whatever.* It's feelings that have been saving my life. You get to drive across Canada. It's a beautiful country. *Whatever* it's doable.

       —American Pie

*****

My dad, there's nobody who means more to me then you do. Helping me through the times when I needed you. You've done so much for me, guiding me through this life that I lead. Holding my hand through the good times and the bad. I love you very much. Because you're my Dad."

—A daughter to her dad
(November 18, 1998)

*****

It's all about presentation. We've been saying that all year. Whether you frame a pitch or *Whatever.*

—Harold Reynolds

There is some magical *Whatever* goes on. That all the changing in theory in the world we never find the answer to.

—Morley Safer

Do you want to go straight home? *Whatever.*

—*Singles*

*****

It is very difficult to go through an entire day without hearing the word *Whatever.* At a big dinner I was at, *Whatever* was said nineteen times in just a couple of hours.

*****

Alex Rodriguez is back, new hip surgery on *Whatever.*

—Orel Hershiser

Tino Martinez hitting 190 or *Whatever* it was.

—Chris Berman

A kick in the back is good, even if you are facing in the right direction."

—Elie Tahari

He kept saying "My friends don't have money." You know people, the richest on the planet. They have to… *Whatever.*

—Dennis Rodman

To my wife, my son, and my soon to be *Whatever* it happens to be, and God.

—Brad Paisley

Everybody is going to be in the Hall of Fame, *Whatever.*

—Harold Reynolds

You remind me of this or you remind me of that or *Whatever* keeps you going or *Whatever.*

—Randy Jackson

She can sing her face off and so can you, *Whatever.*

—Randy Jackson

Although a soldier by profession, I have never felt any sort of fondness for war, and I have never advocated it. Except as a means of peace.

—General Ulysses S. Grant

*****

Preach the positive and coach the negative. Today is a gift so that is why we call it the present.

You need to take care of tomorrow as today will take care of itself. Choice. This is why I do like this saying.

Work as if you don't need the money. Love as you have never been hurt, and dance as no one is watching!

*****

Is there anything that you found that you don't like about being Jewish?

"I think the relatives are a little annoying. I do like being able to tell the Jewish jokes."

—Jerry Seinfeld.

*****

A good leadership style: Excellence without arrogance.

Feeling and perspectives are never wrong, so you need to check the facts.

*****

To love and to be loved is to feel the sun from both sides.

Gordie Howe's response to the question "Why do players always wear a cup but not always a helmet?" "You can always get someone to do your thinking for you."

Please take responsibility for the energy you bring into this space.

—Dr. Taylor

Shakespeare has expressed it best in his poem *Mercy*:

"And the people that are most valuable in your life, are those who make you want to stretch to your fullest potential."

Champions aren't made in the gyms, champions are made from something they have deep inside them—a desire, a dream, a vision.

—Muhammad Ali

If you do what you always did, you'll get what you always got.

—Yogi Berra

Don't cry because it's over. Smile because it happened.

—Dr. Seuss

According to a new survey, women say they feel more comfortable undressing in front of men than they do undressing in front of other women. They say that women are too judgmental, where, of course, men are just grateful.

—Robert DeNiro

Thought for the day: You have all the power there is. There is no one more powerful then you. You just might be aware of it and know it. Don't doubt it. Faith, dummy.

—Willie Nelson

Once you replace negative thoughts with positive ones, you will start having positive results.

—Willie Nelson

If there is no solution to the problem then don't waste time worrying about it. If there is a solution to the problem then don't waste time worrying about it.

—The Dalai Lama

*****

Remember:
If you're not part of the solution,
then you may be part of the problem.

*****

Okay, where were we? Oh yes, here we are. Always
be where you are, I say. And it's always now, and
that's about it. The full significance of the moment
is being realized now, thank you, let's move on.
> —Willie Nelson

When they throw a war and no one shows up, it will
serve as a new beginning of peace on earth. Amen.
> —Willie Nelson

It's better to be decisive than right.
> —Michael Allen

*****

While in all you're knowing, know yourself first.

Most used worst word of 2012: *Whatever!*

Only normal people are the ones you really don't know.

I know where I have been, but I'm not there right now. But I'll
be there again. Whatever!

*****

The 5 Ps

1. Paint the picture. What you need to do is what you focus
   on the longest and it will become the strongest.

2. Program yourself for success. Repetition is 87% of all thoughts are negative. Expand on practice makes for improvement. You need to program your life before it programs you. There are times when you have to become a leader, and at times, you have to be a follower. A leader is able to do both.
3. Partner with powerful people. Be aware of rational illness. Teamwork makes the dream work. Bad people hang around bad people, negative attitudes cluster together. Know your surroundings. Is this where you want to be?
4. Preparation equals power! What got you where you are will not get you to where you want to be.
5. Perception. There are two kinds of sight:
    a. Mind sight
    b. Eyesight

*****

Bisexuality immediately doubles your chances for a date on Saturday night.
—Rodney Dangerfield

If you are gay (not that there's anything wrong with that), and if your partner is the same size as you, you automatically double your wardrobe.
—*Seinfeld*

*****

I am the master of my fate; I am the master of my soul.
Good is the evil of great.

*****

Leadership is heart driven. Remember the definition of management is "getting work done through others."

Ninety percent of management is people and the other ten percent is knowing the job.

It is very important to develop people skills and the ability to communicate with your peers as well as your subordinates.

> The real leader has no need to lead—he is content to point the way.
>
> —Henry Miller

Life is not the way it's supposed to be. It's the way it is! The way we cope with it is what makes the difference. People say "it is what it is." I dislike that saying. Like Pat Summit, an ex-basketball coach, when she said, "It is what it is, but it will be what you make it." RIP, Pat.

*****

> Act as if what you do makes a difference. It does.
> —William James (1842–1910),
> psychologist and author

> Computers are the perfect thing for women who don't feel that men provide them with enough frustration!
>
> —Unknown

> Let us tenderly and kindly cherish, therefore, the means of knowledge. Let us dare to read, think, speak and write.
>
> —John Adams

> Is life so dear, or peace so sweet as to be purchased at the price of chains and slavery? Forbid

it, Almighty God! I know not what course others may take, but as for me, give me liberty, or give me death!

—Patrick Henry

The whole idea of America is that everybody can live their lives the way they choose. When you stick your damn nose in someone else's business, not only are you un-American, but you deserve *Whatever* reaction you get from it.

—Clint Eastwood

You know *that look* women get when they want sex? Me neither.

—Steve Martin

*****

Because I am, you're your best friend. I will always pretend to be your gay lover when you are getting hit on at the bar.

Don't get pissed if people refuse to help you. Be thankful because then you have to complete the task and learn by yourself.

*****

My mother never saw the irony
in calling me a son of a bitch.

—Jack Nicholson

*****

You know you are living in 2013, 2014, and 2015 when:

1. You accidentally enter your PIN number on the microwave.

2. You haven't played solitaire with real cards in years.
3. You have a list of fifteen phone numbers to reach your family of three.
4. You e-mail the person who works at the desk next to you.
5. Your reason for not staying in touch with friends and family is that they don't have e-mail addresses.
6. You pull up in your own driveway and use your cell phone to see if anyone is home to help you carry in the groceries.
7. Every commercial on television has a website at the bottom of the screen.
8. Leaving the house without your cell phone, which you didn't even have the first twenty or thirty (or sixty) years of your life, is now a cause for panic, and you turn around to go and get it.
10. You get up in the morning and go online before getting your coffee.
11. You start tilting your head sideways to smile.
12. You're reading this and nodding and laughing.
13. Even worse, you know exactly to whom you are going to forward this message.
14. You are too busy to notice there was no number nine on this list.

*****

With my old man, I got no respect. I asked him, "How can I get my kite in the air?" He told me to run off a cliff.

I went to a massage parlor. It was self-service.

My wife only has sex with me for a purpose. Last night, she used me to time an egg.

It's tough to stay married. My wife kisses the dog on the lips, yet she won't drink from my glass! Last night, my wife met me at the front door. She was wearing a sexy negligee. The only trouble was, she was coming home.

A girl phoned me and said, "Come on over. There's nobody home." I went over. Nobody was home!

A hooker once told me she had a headache.

If it weren't for pickpockets, I'd have no sex life at all.

I was making love to this girl and she started crying. "Are you going to hate yourself in the morning?" She said, "No, I hate myself now."

I knew a girl so ugly they use her in prisons to cure sex offenders.

My wife is such a bad cook. If we leave dental floss in the kitchen, the roaches would hang themselves.

I'm so ugly I stuck my head out the window and got arrested for mooning.

The other day I came home and a guy was jogging naked.
I asked him, "Why?"
He said, "Because you came home early."

My wife's such a bad cook, the dog begs for Alka-Seltzer.

I know I'm not sexy. When I put my underwear on, I can hear the Fruit of the Loom guys giggling.

My wife is such a bad cook that in my house we pray after the meal.

My wife likes to talk to me during sex. Last night, she called me from a hotel.

My family was so poor that if I hadn't been born a boy, I wouldn't have had anything to play with.

It's been a rough day. I got up this morning and put a shirt on and a button fell off. I picked up my briefcase, and the handle came off. I'm afraid to go to the bathroom.

I was such an ugly kid! When I played in the sandbox, the cat kept covering me up.

I could tell my parents hated me. My bath toys were a toaster and radio.

I was such an ugly baby that my mother never breastfed me. She told me that she only liked me as a friend.

I'm so ugly my father carried around a picture of the kid that came with his wallet.

When I was born, the doctor came into the waiting room and said to my father, "I'm sorry. We did everything we could, but he pulled through anyway."

I'm so ugly my mother had morning sickness *after* I was born.

I remember the time that I was kidnapped and they sent a piece of my finger to my father. He said he wanted more proof.

Once, when I was lost, I saw a policeman and asked him to help me find my parents. I said to him, "Do you think we'll ever find them?" He said, "I don't know, kid. There's so many places they can hide."

My wife made me join a bridge club. I jump off next Tuesday.

I'm so ugly, I once worked in a pet shop, and people kept asking how big I'd get.

I went to see my doctor. "Doctor, every morning when I get up and I look in the mirror, I feel like throwing up. What's wrong with me?" He said, "Nothing. Your eyesight is perfect."

I went to the doctor because I'd swallowed a bottle of sleeping pills. My doctor told me to have a few drinks and get some rest.

Some dog I got. We call him Egypt because in every room, he leaves a pyramid. His favorite bone is in my arm. Last night, he went on the paper four times. Three of those times I was reading it.

One year, they wanted to make me a poster boy...for birth control.

My uncle's dying wish was to have me sitting in his lap. He was in the electric chair.

And that's why we miss Rodney Dangerfield.

*****

I dive in really deep, because I think leadership in crisis is about getting down in the trenches... there's no substitute for being there.
                                        —Meg Whitman, CEO of Quibi

No one has more sh———t on their to-do list than a kid who's just told its bedtime.

Having any sense is not a gift. It's a punishment because you deal with everyone who doesn't have it.

Stress is caused by being here, and wanting to be there.

—Eckhart Tolle

Getting lost is never a waste of time.

Don't wait. The time will never be just right.

—Napoleon Hill

People who love to eat, are always the best people. Imagine that!

—Julia Child

*****

Life Lessons from Robin Williams.

1. Sometimes the best response is no response.
    "Even fools seem smart when they are quiet."
2. There is a lesson in everything.
    "You will always have bad times but they will wake you up to the stuff you weren't paying attention to."
3. Keep alive the things that make you feel alive.
    "You're only given a little spark of madness. You mustn't lose it."
4. Everyone has a story we know nothing about.
    "I think the saddest people always try their hardest to make people happy because they know what it's like to feel absolutely worthless, and they don't want anyone else to feel like that.
5. You can change the world.
    "No matter what people tell you, words and ideas can change the world."

*****

A friend is one of the nicest things you can have.

In my next life, I'm coming back with money and looks, instead of all this sparkling personality bullshit.

Let your smile change the world. Don't let the world change your smile.

Some people just couldn't be nice even if a unicorn shoved a fairy wand up their butt while Judy Garland stood there singing "Somewhere over the Rainbow."

WHATEVER

Every time you wake up and realize you're alive and healthy, be thankful.

—Jeff Heinemann

*****

Three things you need to give up if you want to be happy:

1. Limiting beliefs.
2. Dwelling on the past.
3. Worrying about the future.

*****

Vodka is made from potatoes.
Potatoes are a vegetable.
Vodka is a salad.
Great! I'll have a salad for dinner!

*****

Despite everything, no one can dictate who you are to other people.

—Prince

I spent half my money on gambling, alcohol, and wild women. The other half I wasted.

—W. C. Fields

Treat Earth well. It was not given to you by your parents. "It was lent to you by your children."

—Anonymous

Teamwork divides the task and multiplies the success!

—Unknown

*****

A boss I had once told me to just slit my wrists now. Because if I knew what was going to happen to me the rest of my life, it would be easier and I would not have to deal with anything.
Do your personal maintenance every day!

*****

Power of Positivity

Let go of toxic people in your life.
Let go of regretting past mistakes.
Let go of the need to be right.
Let go of feeling sorry for yourself.
Let go of negative self-talk.
Let go of the need to impress others.

*****

The secret of living well is eat half, walk double, laugh triple, and love without measures.

—Tibetan proverb

*****

Stop complaining. Being an adult is easy. Pay your bills, don't smoke meth, keep a few close friends, wear deodorant, and tip your waitresses and bartenders! Just let go, enjoy, and be happy!

*****

Let go of how you thought your life should be,
and embrace the life that is trying to work its way
into consciousness.

—Caroline Myss

*****

Mom's Sayings

"If everyone jumped off a cliff, would you do it too?"
  "Don't talk with your mouth full."
  "Clean up your room. It looks like a tornado hit it."
  "Do you think I was born yesterday?"
  "Because I said so. That's why!"
  "Money doesn't grow on trees."
  "Look at me when I am talking to you."
  "Don't use that tone of voice with me."
  "Don't make me come in there."
  "I'm coming in there right now!"
  "Don't make me come in there again."
  "Who do you think you are?"
  "Just wait until your father gets home."
  "Stop fighting or I'll turn this car right around."
  "What part of no do you not understand?"
  "I don't care who started it."
  "Put your Game Boy down."
  "Your face is going to freeze like that."
  "Your hands are not broken."
  "No one said life is fair."
  "Beds are for sleeping not for jumping on."
  "Eat your vegetables."
  "I don't know is not an answer."
  "I wish you knew your schoolwork as well as you know the
words to the songs."

"Because you were sick and could not go to school, you cannot go out and play."

"Don't make me come into the back seat!"

"Get off the computer."

"No cell phones at the table."

"Don't drink from the hose."

"No swimming in the canal."

"Talk to the hand because my ears are not listening."

"You're like a cornfield. You have big ears."

"Turn the lights out when you leave the room."

"Change the channel. That's not for kids."

"Until you get your homework done, I'm taking away…"

"No playing ball in the house."

"How many did I miss that you can remember?"

*****

What a man says to his wife (this may be a country western song): No expectations, no disappointments.

Every day and year of your life, you will need a different version of yourself.

Take vacations: You can't always make money, but you can always make memories.

*****

Passion!

Passion is when you apply more energy than what is required to reach an accomplishment or excitement.

Passion is ambition that is materialized into action.

*****

Successful people have a sense of gratitude. Unsuccessful people have a sense of entitlement.
—Stephen Atchison

Teams should be able to act with the same unity of purpose and focus as well as a well-motivated individual.
—Bill Gates

We must reject the idea that every time a law is broken, society is guilty rather than the law-breaker. It is time to restore the American precept that each individual is accountable for his actions.
—Ronald Regan (1968)

Something wonderful is about to happen. Do what makes you happy.

I may be drunk, miss, but in the morning I will be sober, and you will still be ugly.
—Winston Churchill

Dogs have owners. Cats have staff.

Separate the people from the ideas people have.

The curious mind stays agile, innovative and competitive. With our native human curiosity and culture of collaboration, there are few limits to what we can achieve.

The Jewish year is 5776. The Chinese year is 4714. This means the Jews had to exist 1,062 years without Chinese food, a time known as the Dark Ages.

Overeating does not cause obesity. Obesity causes overeating.

Statue of David
returns to Italy after
3 years in the USA

Distance doesn't separate people. Silence does.
—Jeff Hood

It ain't what you know that gets you in trouble.
It's what you know for sure that ain't so.
—Mark Twain

*****

Cite somebody's work and recognize them. Give them a complement. Make them feel better about their accomplishments. They will feel better about themselves. They also now know that you care about them and their work.

We love kids, but please keep yours at your table! Unattended children will be handed a Red Bull and a cattle prod.

Great Wall of China:
Can you see the little soldier going up to the emperor and saying, "You want me to do what? You want me to build what?"

Live every day like it's your last because one day
you will be right.

—Mahammad Ali

You get out of life what you have the courage to
ask for.

—Oprah

Whatever is rude and dismissive? *Whatever* was in the top five
words in 2013 that Americans were fed up with and wanted to say
bye-bye to for the most annoying word for five straight years.

*****

*****

Part of the "Rat Pack"

No one is born a great cook. One learns by doing.
—Julia Child

*****

Expect what you inspect!!! No surprises.

*****

It's more important to be good than to be great.
—John-John Kennedy

It's not as important to be a member of a country club. It's more important to know a member.
—KD

The needs of a few do not out way the needs of many.
—Warren

*****

Some great football quotes.

Gentlemen, it is better to have died a small boy
than to fumble the football.
—John Heisman

I make my practices real hard because if a player
is a quitter, I want him to quit in practice, not in
a game.
—Bear Bryant, Alabama

It isn't necessary to see a good tackle. You can hear it!
—Knute Rockne, Notre Dame

At Georgia Southern, we don't cheat. That costs
money, and we don't have any.
—Erik Russell, Georgia Southern

The man who complains about the way the ball
bounces is likely to be the one who dropped it.
—Lou Holtz, Arkansas-Notre Dame

When you win, nothing hurts.
—Joe Namath, Alabama

A school without football is in danger of deterio-
rating into a medieval study hall.
—Frank Leahy, Notre Dame

There's nothing that cleanses your soul like getting the hell kicked out of you.
—Woody Hayes, Ohio State

I don't expect to win enough games to be put on
NCAA probation. I just want to win enough to
warrant an investigation.
—Bob Devaney, Nebraska

In Alabama, an atheist is someone who doesn't believe in Bear Bryant.

—Wally Butts, Georgia

I never graduated from Iowa. But I was only there for two terms—Truman's and Eisenhower's.

—Alex Karras, Iowa

My advice to defensive players is to take the shortest route to the ball, and arrive in a bad humor.

—Bowden Wyatt, Tennessee

I could have been a Rhodes scholar except for my grades.

—Duffy Daugherty, Michigan State

Always remember Goliath was a forty-point favorite over David.

—Shug Jordan, Auburn

I asked Darrell Royal, the coach of the Texas Longhorns, why he didn't recruit me. He said, "Well, Walt, we took a look at you, and you weren't any good."

—Walt Garrison, Oklahoma State

Son, you've got a good engine, but your hands aren't on the steering wheel.

—Bobby Bowden, Florida State

Football is *not* a contact sport. It is a collision sport. Dancing *is* a contact sport.

—Duffy Daugherty, Michigan State

After USC lost 51–0 to Notre Dame, his post-game message to his team was "All those who need showers, take them."
—John McKay, USC

If lessons are learned in defeat, our team is getting a great education.
—Murray Warmath, Minnesota

The only qualifications for a lineman are to be big and dumb. To be a back, you only have to be dumb.
—Knute Rockne, Notre Dame

We live one day at a time and scratch where it itches.
—Darrell Royal, Texas

We didn't tackle well today, but we made up for it by not blocking.
—John McKay, USC

I've found that prayers work best when you have big players.
—Knute Rockne, Notre Dame

Ohio State's Urban Meyer on one of his players: "He doesn't know the meaning of the word *fear*. In fact, I just saw his grades and he doesn't know the meaning of a lot of words."

Why do Tennessee fans wear orange? So they can dress that way for the game on Saturday, go hunting on Sunday, and pick up trash on Monday.

What does the average Alabama player get on his SATs? Drool.

How many Michigan State freshmen football players does it take to change a lightbulb? None. That's a sophomore course.

How did the Auburn football player die from drinking milk? The cow fell on him.

Two Texas A&M football players were walking in the woods. One of them said, "Look, a dead bird." The other looked up in the sky and said, "Where?"

What do you say to a Florida State University football player dressed in a three-piece suit? "Will the defendant please rise?"

If three Rutgers football players are in the same car, who is driving? The police officer.

How can you tell if a Clemson football player has a girlfriend? There's tobacco juice on both sides of the pickup truck.

What do you get when you put thirty-two Arkansas cheerleaders in one room? A full set of teeth.

University of Michigan Coach Jim Harbaugh is only going to dress half of his players for the game this week.

The other half will have to dress themselves.

How is the Kansas football team like an opossum? They play dead at home and get killed on the road.

Why did the Tennessee linebacker steal a police car? He saw 911 on the side and thought it was a Porsche.

How do you get a former Illinois football player off your porch? Pay him for the pizza.

*****

Steve Young, Earl Campbell, Ken Stabler. Three of the great ones!

Third place winner 1992 SLC. No money,
just a cup, as no gambling in Utah.

*****

Believe in something And the universe is on its
way to being changed. Because you've changed,
by believing. Once you've changed, other things
start to follow. Isn't that the way it works?
— Diane Duane

Life is like a coin. You can spend it anyway you
want to, but you can only spend it once.
— Unknown

A person without a sense of humor is like a wagon
without springs. It's jolted by every pebble on the
road.
— Henry Ward Beecher

Procrastination is like a credit card: It's a lot of
fun until you get the bill.
— Christopher Parker

Progress is impossible without change, and those
who cannot change their minds cannot change
anything.
— Aristotle

Your greatest display of strength in life comes at
the time when you're able to help someone else
while you're going through your own storm.

Calm down mechanic guy. Just here for an oil change. If I wanted to know about all the other stuff wrong with my car, I'd turn down the radio.

Compromise needs compromise. To get cooperation, you have to give cooperation.

You may all go to hell. And I will go to Texas.
—Davy Crockett

All we have to do is to decide is what to do with the time that is given to us.
—J.R.R. Tolkien

You can't get much done in life if you only work on the days when you feel good.
—Jerry West

One measure of a man is what he does when he has nothing to do.

—Robert Edison Fulton Jr.

Mentors, by far, are the most important aspect of business.

—Daymond John

Grow through what you go through!

The only person you should try to be better than is the person you were yesterday.

To my wife, I am not perfect, I'll annoy you, say stupid things and may tease you. But you know that I love you now and always will.

*****

Funny but not funny.

What is funny for some is not funny for all!

Follow your soul. It knows the way.

Wherever you go, go with all your heart.

Think outside the *box*!

Just put on your big-girl panties, and deal with it!

I'll please have a café mocha vodka valium latte, tall. To go, please.
Sometimes having coffee with your best friend is all you need!

Please watch out for each other and love and forgive everybody. It's a good life and enjoy it.

Original Sorry! card from the original game, invented in 1957.

*****

Reality check. Sorry there is no Prince Charming. Just take the shoes, please.

In life, it's not where you go, it's who you travel with.

> —On-Site Travel Directors,
> Charles Schultz

Together is my favorite place to be! Disney life, happy wife. You're never too old for Disney.

*****

That's what I do. I drink and I know thinks! Oops... Did I roll my eyes out loud?

*****

If stress burned calories, I would be a size 3.

The road ahead is long, drive safely.
—Chinese cookie

May all your wrinkles be laugh lines.

It's not who you are that defines you. It's what you do that defines you.

Pressure is a privilege.
—Billie Jean King

*****

You know how to manipulate a crowd.
Democrats or Republicans: which one?
"A bunch of rich people, convincing poor people to vote for the rich people by telling the poor people that the other rich people are the reason they are poor."
I'm confused.

When I was very young growing up in the sixties, my dad said that all the politicians are a bunch of crooks, and they just haven't gotten caught yet! How true is this today?

Politics:

Poli meaning many tics, meaning blood-sucking insects from the Greeks.

> With age comes experience. With experience comes wisdom. With wisdom comes judgement.
> —Joe Biden

*****

Life is calling. I must go. What is life but one grand adventure?

I don't know where I am going, but I am going.

I just spent two weeks hanging out with myself, and I am so sorry to every person I have ever spent time with.

Did you get your shirt yet?

*****

Start every day with a smile, and you can get it over with.

—W. C. Fields

What happens is not as important as how you react to what happens.

—Thaddeus Golas

To Life!!!

It's nice to be important. But it's more important to be nice.

In making others happy,
You will be happy too.
For the happiness you give away,
returns to shine on you.

—Helen Steiner Rice

Joy that's shared is a joy made double!

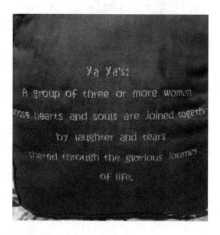

Ya Ya's:
A group of three or more women
whose hearts and souls are joined together
by laughter and tears
shared through the glorious journey
of life.

Ya Yas: A group of three or more women whose hearts and souls are joined together by laughter and tears, shared through the glorious journey of life.

*****

To find a rainbow, you must weather the storm.

Enjoy the little things, for one day you may look back, and realize they were the big things.

If you have positive thinking, then you have a beautiful life.

—Fran Marcus

Let your faith be Bigger than your fear.

*****

Family Rules:

- Share.
- Do your best.
- Speak kind words.
- Be patient.
- Forgive
- No whining.
- Dream big!

*****

Rules for today:

1. A little more laughter
2. A little less worry

3. A little more kindness
4. A little less hurry

*****

Why fit in when you were born to stand out!

*****

What exactly is in your sneeze?

That sneeze that blasted out of your nose contains 5,000 water droplets, along with assorted mucous, bacteria, viruses, and other debris, all traveling at 100 miles per hour. The drops can travel up to 15 feet. In ancient Rome, people said "God bless you" when somebody sneezed. We don't know why this practice began, but we continue the custom to this day. It may possibly because you heart may skip a beat when you sneeze and they say "God bless you" so your heart will continue beating?

Your nose can identify 50,000 different scents. Not sure how many a dog would have. Okay, I looked it up, and they have 300,000,000 olfactory receptors in their noses and humans have approximately 6 million. Cats have about twice as many than us. Dogs win!

*****

Your lungs breathe in between 2,100 and 2,400 gallons of air each day.

Your brain accounts for about 2% of your body weight but uses some 20% of the oxygen and calories you consume. Where do some men keep their brain?

Your heart beats 100,000 times a day, 40 million times a year, and 3 billion times over an average life. Okay, start counting.

Every time you take a step, you use 200 different muscles. Start walking more!

Start to create the stories you will never stop sharing!

Hold on to doubt!
Curiosity-based decision-making, not fear-based decision-making.

*****

Practical tips for leaders:

1. Model aspirations between your ideas and yourself. Criticize your own ideas.
2. Don't fear the open question. There is always an answer.
3. Make the best decision you can when you have to make the decision. Don't spend your energy second-guessing.
4. Find something to love in everyone you work with.

*****

When we explore, we are asking questions about ourselves we are looking for our potential.

Curiosity is in our genes. The curious mind stays agile, innovative, and competitive.

With our native human curiosity and a culture of collaboration, there are few limits to what we can achieve.

Some people want it to happen, some wish it would happen, others make it happen!

Your sense of humor is a joy to all!

Remember that smiles and laughter are the universal languages.

*****

Did you know?

- Your nostrils take turns inhaling. You breathe through one nostril for three to four hours and then switch to the other one.
- Your bladder can hold about two cups of urine comfortably. Does beer count?

- Why does beer go through you quicker than water? That's because it doesn't have to stop to change colors!
- Feet sweat because there are about 250,000 pores on their soles that produce a quarter cup of liquid each day.

*****

Your Birthday Suit.

Skin is the largest organ in your body, weighing in at about seven pounds. It's alive and constantly changing. In fact, you shed flakes of skin and grow new skin cells every day. You get a whole new layer of skin every twenty-eight days. Tiny pores in your skin contain oil and sweat glands to keep your skin elastic and cool as well as protect you from bacteria. Who knew?

*****

DISTANCE
JLS

Sometimes distance makes the heart grow fonder,
And sometimes it feels like a test.
Sometimes it breeds enthusiasm, and sometimes it
Loses its zest.
As time goes by there is no
Doubt that our love has really grown;
But sometimes communication
Makes the heart feel sad and feel alone.
I wouldn't give our relationship up for anything,
But life does get it in the way.
I hope you understand this poem
And have a wonderful day!

*****

Sometimes life is only one tent away from a full-blown circus.

Mothers are the angels who lift us up when our wings forget how to fly.

The best antiques are old friends! New friends are great, but old friends know where you have been.

Raising teenagers is like nailing Jell-O to a tree.

Notice: Our prices are subject to change depending on customer's attitude.

Remember when sex, drugs, and rock 'n' roll meant something other than Sunday, antidepressants, and turn it down?

You know you have moved to Florida when your new BFF is the pharmacist.

Some days you just have to ask "as if…" but some days you just may say WTF!!!

Just drink until she is cute. How come they all start to look better as the bar is closing?

Eat, sleep, wine, repeat. Or just skip the first two.

For my soul mate, and just in case you ever may wonder how I feel about you. Look in the mirror. In the reflection you see the person I want to spend my whole life with, the one I love more than words can say. The one who makes me happy, the one I want to grow old with. So if you ever have any doubt who makes my life complete, look into the mirror and you will see. I love you today and always.

—Suzy Toronto@suzyToronto.com

Your focus determines your reality.
—*Star Wars: Phantom Menace*

*****

	Cost of Living	
	1969	2016
New House	$15,525.00	$218,000.00
Average Income	$8,547.00 per year	$51,939.00
New Car Average	$3,378.00	$33,560.00
Average Rent	$135.00 per month	$1,001.00
Tuition at Harvard	$2,000.00 per year	$43,280.00
Movie Ticket	$1.50	$8.42
Gasoline	0.35 per gallon	$2.46
First Class Stamp	0.06	0.47

	Food Prices Average	
	1969	2016
Granulated Sugar (5 lbs)	$0.76	$3.48
Gallon of Milk	$1.26	$2.32
Coffee, Ground (1 lb)	$0.96	$10.00
Bacon (1 lb)	$0.76	$5.60
Eggs (1 doz.)	$0.40	$1.66
Ground Hamburger	$0.57	$4.02

As Bob Dylan said, "The Times, They are A-Changin'."

At times it takes a village!

A great *Star Trek* line:
Hey, where's the money I need to pay for this.
Oh, we don't use any money now, everything is
for the betterment of mankind.

*****

Plan A is always my first choice, the one where
everything works out. But more often than not, I
find myself dealing with the upside-down version
where nothing goes as it should. It is at this point
that the real test of my character comes in. Do
I sink or do I swim? Do I wallow in self-pity, or
do I simply shift gears and make the best of the
situation? The choice is mine. Life is really about
how you handle plan B.
—Suzy Toronto@suzytoronto.com

If plan A doesn't work, there are twenty-five more
letters in the alphabet.

Grace isn't a little prayer you say before receiving
a meal. It's a way of life.

*****

"I pledge allegiance to the flag of the United States of America, and
to the republic for which it stands, one nation under God, indivisi-
ble, with liberty and justice for all."
Just in case you forgot the words.

*****

Good morning. This is God. I will be handling all of your problems today.

*****

Some great words to live by:

Life is too short.
Break the rules.
Forgive quickly.
Be nice to yourself.
Laugh every day.
Love deeply.

*****

Order the good wine, for tomorrow you may be dead.

—Glenn Frey

*****

Does walking to get my wine refilled count for my steps for the day and also count as my cardio exercise?

Sometimes the wrong choices brings us to the right places.

Don't stumble over something behind you! Life is like a hot bath, it feels good, but the longer you stay in, the more *wrinkled* you get.

*****

Marriage is a relationship where one person is always right, and the other is the husband.

Happy wife, happy life.

Little by little *Whatever* the weather, friends and flowers grow together.

We're all ignorant. Just about different things.
—Mark Twain

Look for the beauty, listen with love, live with intention.

Folks who have no vices, have no virtues.
—Abe Lincoln

You must do things you think you cannot do.
—Eleanor Roosevelt

I know I'm in my own world. It's okay. They know me here.

Kids are our future. Not your kids. Better ones.

Behold the turtle. He makes progress only
when he sticks his neck out.

There's this little elf that lives on the shelf in my house and it comes alive every night. Can you please get that creepy bastard out of my house?

Absence makes the heart grow fonder. It also tends to get you fired.

A group of kids is called a migraine.

The work that never ends is COURAGE!

Happiness is a journey, not a destination.

Whatever you are, be a good one.

The really happy person, is the one who can enjoy.

Life is what you make it. Always has been and always will be.

*****

Words of Wisdom for My Son.

Think BIG. If that doesn't work, think bigger. Be nice. Play fair. Forgive everyone. Rise by lifting others. Nothing is as strong as a man who is tender or as weak as a man who thinks he has to be tough. It's okay to ask for directions. Trust your crazy ideas. I gave you winks so I could watch you soar, so jump even if you have to learn how to fly on the way down.

Life is all about how you handle plan B. I always said one day I would have to let you go, but I lied. I'm never letting go. And remember, I believe in you. Always have, always will. I think you are absolutely over-the-top amazing. DON'T ever forget it.

—Suzy Toronto@suzytoronto.com

*****

To My Granddaughter,

Few moments in my life have been greater than the very first time I held you in my arms. As you took a deep breath and sighed one of your sweet baby sighs, you took my breath away. You were such a great, big miracle, all packaged up in the cutest little, teeny tiny body, and you just seemed to smile all the time.

Holding you instantly put me in my "happy place" and became my very most favorite thing to do in the history of forever! Your mom practically had to pry you out of my arms.

As you grew, you became my favorite "hello" and my hardest "goodbye," for in you I see eyes full of adventure and dreams, a mind spinning with unlimited possibilities for the future, and a body filled with unbound energy and enthusiasm. You are my posterity...and my JOY.

Folks often say that if they knew grandchildren were so much fun, they'd have had them first. I agree...especially when it comes to you.

Oh, my granddaughter! I am so proud of you.

—Suzy Toronto@suzytoronto.com

*****

I must hurry and catch them. For I am their leader.

—John M, USN retired captain

"Rule no. 1 for wearing a speedo: If you can't see it, you can't wear it." (Is this the only rule?)

If everyone did that, we would all have to see a psychiatrist...well...*Whatever.*

—George

"These pretzels are making me thirsty."

—Kramer

When its yellow let it mellow. When it's brown flush it down.

*****

Remember, everyone comes with baggage. Find someone who will help you unpack, and you can help unpack them!

A man's success has a lot to do with the kind of women he chooses to have in his life.

*****

Flight attendant: "Do you want breakfast?"
"What are my choices?"
"Your choice is yes or no!"

*****

NAVY (Never Again Volunteer Yourself)

Navy SEAL motto: The only good day was yesterday.

Live hand in hand and together we will stand on a threshold of a dream.
                                        —Moody Blues

Live hand in hand and together we will stand on a threshold of a dream. Come walk with me.
                                        —Words used in my wedding vows

*****

From a twelve-year-old boy
Anonymous

Watch your thoughts
They become weird.
Watch your words
They become actions.
Watch your actions
They become habits.
Watch your habits
It becomes your destiny.

*****

These mountains that you are carrying, you were
only supposed to climb them.
—Najwa Zebian

A river cuts through rock. Not because of its
power, but because of its persistence.
—Unknown

As long as I live, you will live. As long as I live,
you will be loved. As long as I live, you will be
remembered.
—Unknown

*****

A lady is sitting in a boat reading a book at a popular fishing spot.
The game warden comes to her and says, "Can I see your fishing license?"
"I do not have one, and I am just reading."

"Seeing all the fishing equipment you have in the boat, you might go fishing, so I have to write you a ticket since you possibly might go fishing and you do not have a license."

"If you write me a ticket, I may have to sue you for sexual harassment."

"But I have done nothing to sexually harass you."

"Yes, I know but you have all the equipment to possibly do so."

Yeah, *Whatever!*

*****

Murphy's Other 15 Laws

1. Light travels faster than sound. This is why some people appear bright until you hear them speak.
2. A fine is a tax for doing wrong. A tax is a fine for doing well.
3. He who laughs last thinks slowest.
4. A day without sunshine is like, well, night.
5. Change is inevitable, except from a vending machine.
6. Those who live by the sword get shot by those who don't.
7. Nothing is foolproof to a sufficiently talented fool.
8. The 50-50-90 rule. Anytime you have a fifty-fifty chance of getting something right, there's a ninety percent probability you'll get it wrong.
9. It is said that if you line up all the cars in the world end to end, someone would be stupid enough to try to pass them.
10. If the shoe fits, get another one just like it.
11. The things that come to those who wait may be the things left by those who got there first.
12. Give a man a fish and he will eat for a day. Teach a man to fish and he will sit in a boat all day drinking beer.
13. Flashlight: a case for holding dead batteries.
14. God gave you toes as a device for finding furniture in the dark.

15. When you go into court, you are putting yourself in the hands of twelve people, who weren't smart enough to get out of jury duty.

*****

Clothes and manners do not make the man, but when he is made, they greatly improve his experience.
                                            —Arthur Ash

The best color in the whole world is the one that looks good on you.
                                            —Coco Chanel

Over the years, I have learned that what is important in a dress, is the woman who is wearing it.
                                            —Yves Saint Laurent

Cinderella: proof that that a new pair of shoes can change your life.

If the shoe fits, buy it in every color.

Life is short, buy the shoes!

Wine doesn't have many vitamins. That's why I have to drink a lot.

Housework won't kill you, but why take the chance?

If you want what you never had, you've got to do what you have never done!

Be curious. Use your wits. Don't be a picky eater. Take time to play. Soar above it all. Make your whole voice heard. Don't let life ruffle your feathers!

—Hermit's Rest, Grand Canyon

One must always aim beyond the target. One must aim a long way. Our whole life, our whole spirit travels with the arrow. And when the arrow has been released, it is never the end.

—Awa Kenzo

Be not afraid of life. Believe that life is worth living and your belief will help create the fact.

—William James

Out where the hands clap
A little stronger.
Out where the smile wells
A little longer.
That's where the West begins.

—Arthur Chapman

Don't cry because it's over. Smile because it happened.

—Dr. Seuss

Look back to learn and look forward to succeed!

She's not really dead, if we find a way to remember her.

—*Seinfeld*

Golf is a deceptively simple and endlessly complicated game. It is without a doubt the greatest game mankind has ever invented.

—Arnold Palmer

Some people may only like you if you fit inside their box. Don't be afraid to shove the box up their ass.

The happiest people don't have the best of everything, they just have the best of everything they have.

—Unknown

What did the saggy boob say to the other? We'd better perk up or people will think we're nuts!

It's not the load that breaks you down. It's the way you carry it.

—Lena Horne

I'm getting old… I got out of bed and I had chest pains… I looked down and I realized I was standing on my nipples.

TEAM: Together Everyone Achieves More! There is *no I* in team. Be careful, there is an *m* and *e*…me.

Looking for leadership? Look in the mirror.

—Peter Block

A leader is a dealer in hope.

—Napoleon Bonaparte

Vision is the art of seeing thinks invisible.
                    —Jonathan Swift

There are no shortcuts to any place worth going.
                    —Beverly Sills

Don't wait for your ship to come in. Swim after it.
                    —Jonathan Winters

Most things are difficult, before they are easy.
                    —Thomas Fuller
                    (But now we just YouTube it.)

We never know the worth of water till the well runs dry.
                    —Thomas Fuller

When you drink from a well, remember the men who dug the well.
                    —Brad Paisley

Act like you are invincible. Know you are not.

Fail to honor people, and they will fail to honor you.
                    —Lao-tzu

I praise loudly. I blame softly.
                    —Catherine the Great

The more you say, the less they remember.
                    —Anatole France

It's not what happens when you are there… It's what happens when you're not.

—Ken Blanchard

*****

A good manager is determined on how their business runs when they are not there! Not to mention good parenting.

*****

Authority is a poor substitute for leadership.

—John Luther (Listen and lead!)

There's always room at the top but even more room at the bottom.

—Daniel Webster

Everyone seems to want to climb the ladder to success until they get to the top and realize there is nowhere to sit down.

Why not go out on a limb? Isn't that where the fruit is?

—Frank Scully

Enjoy the process but crave the goal.

We will either find a way…or make one.

—Hannibal

Be not afraid of greatness.

—William Shakespeare

Real leaders are ordinary people with extraordinary determination.

—Anonymous

*****

What we have or haven't learned in the past two thousand years:

The budget should be balanced, public debt should be reduced, the arrogance of officialdom (an organization of government departments) should be tempered and controlled, and the assistance to foreign lands should be curtailed lest Rome becomes bankrupt. People must again learn to work, instead of being on public assistance.

How true are these words today that (were spoken over two thousand years ago?) I guess they had issues also back then…

—Cicero (55 BC)

Act before it happens so you won't have to re-act after it happens. So true!!!

It's easier to keep up than it is to catch up.

If you haven't walked in another person's shoes, you can't judge them.

When you have an idea on something that needs to be done by someone else, ask their opinion on how we should accomplish the task. By doing this and using their input, they become a part of the solution and take pride in completing the task, as they have taken ownership of the task and the solution. And then you have a "we decision."

Learn from things you did wrong and improve on the things you did right. When you become aware, you become responsible to act.

*****

We can never help another without helping ourselves.

—Ralph Waldo Emerson

Always try and live one step below your means, and you will feel wealthy all the time.

—Orson Bean

*****

You cannot get what you never had if you are not willing to do what you have never done.

Become a DWIT (Do What It Takes)!

When you can't see, become a better listener. Let's all become better listeners!

*****

Whether you think you can or you think you can't, you're right.

—Henry Ford

****

Confidence exceeds competence.

Every busines talks about serving the customer better. But as you know, they do not always do what they said they would. Remember we are just people helping people, serving one another as our own customers.

Customer service is not just a department, it is your attitude. So is helping family friends and others.

Anticipate the needs of others. Help someone out when you can.

*****

Many of life's failures are men who did not realize how close they were to success when they
gave up.
                              —Henry Ford

                    *****

People don't care how much you know until they know how much
you care.

   Never let emotion trump reason! Remember at times some
things are said in the heat of battle but also, so can be your actions.

                    *****

The beauty of this book is, that it is still being written as it is written.

                    *****

Everybody has a first day. It all matters what you
do next.

There's just too much to see waiting in front of
me, and I know that I just can't go wrong.
                              —Jimmy Buffett

If you cannot forgive, you should dig two graves.
One for you and one for the other.
                              —Chinese proverb

                    *****

Sometimes what is right is not necessarily best.
   The answer you sometimes get may not be the answer you
were expecting. That is now when you have to deal with reality.

You may have expected to go in another direction, but now you have to change course. Adjust your thinking and embrace your best possible results.

Embrace change even when the change slaps you in the face. (Every change can be good if you make it that way.)

Changing and Turning

The circle of life, we all have a turn.

Remember that we all will have a turn. As the Byrds' sang and Pete Seeger wrote, "to everything turn! turn! turn! / There is a season turn, turn, turn / And a time to every purpose / under heaven."

Even though these words are from back in the 60s, how true they are today and will be true tomorrow! Like when a friend is on vacation and you say "What about me? How come I can't go?" Well, it is not your turn. It may be next week or next year but not now. Be happy for them. Be glad for their fortunes. You will get your turn. When did we stop talking about me? Well, it's not always about you. Be happy for them, and you will get your turn.

Eat two meals a day. (That's all you need.)

Work as long as you can. That money is going to come in handy, and yes, the government will thank you!

Help others. The more you do for others, the better shape you're in.

We're all going to die. Some people are afraid of dying. (Never be afraid to die because you're born to die.) You never hear of any unhappy customers.

Are humans the only species that knows they are going to die?

*****

Prediction is awfully hard to do, especially if it is about the future.

—Yogi Berra

*****

If it is true that almost everything we become and accomplish in life is with and through other people, then we have the ability to create rapport with people. It is the most important skill we can learn.

*****

Attitude is a little thing that makes a big difference.

—Winston Churchill

There are no traffic jams along the extra mile.

—Roger Staubach

I fear regret more then I fear failure.

—Lisa B

Your character is tested when you're up against it.

—Dick Vermeil

May the road rise to meet you.
May the wind always be at your back.
May the sun shine warmly upon your face.
May the rains fall softly upon your fields.
And until we met again,
May God hold you in the palm of his hands.

—Irish blessing

I can sum it up like this: Thank God for the game
of golf.

—Arnold Palmer

Golf is a game that is played on a five-inch
course—the distance between your ears.

—Bobby Jones

*****

If you think you are outclassed, you are;
You've got to think high to rise.
You've got to be sure of yourself before
You can even win a prize.

Life's battles don't always go
To the stronger or faster man;
But soon or late the man who wins
Is the man who thinks he can!

—Arnold Palmer

*****

Remember when you get some bills in the mail.
If they are important enough, they will send you
another.

May there always be work for your hands to do.
May your purse always hold a coin or two.
May the sun always shine on your window pane.
May a rainbow be certain to follow each rain.
May the hands of a friend always be near you.
May God fill your heart with gladness and cheer.

—Irish blessing

Retirement: You get twice the husband but half as much money.

If all I have taught you is to block and tackle, then I have failed as a coach.
—Ed Thomas

The simplest path to a Super Bowl is if you have a franchise quarterback.
—Chris Collinsworth

Some men see things as they are and say "Why?" I dream things that never were and say why not.
—George Bernard Shaw

We must become the change we want to be.
—Gandhi

*****

Respect is like air. You don't think about it until it is gone.

Respect is something you don't think about until it is gone, and then that's all you think about.

It's more important to be respected as a person than to be respected by your position.

Respect the person, not the position.

Always do the right thing for the right reasons.

No pity party for the self-inflicted.

*****

Talk is cheap because supply exceeds demand.

No war plan ever met an enemy and remained unchanged.
——General Tommy Franks

Take care of the little things and the big things will take care of themselves.
——Joe Paterno

You don't do things right once in a time, so do it all the time.
——Vince Lombardi

There's nothing ugly about a W.
——Urban Meyer

Life is tough, and even tougher when you're stupid.
——John Wayne

If the mother is sick, addicted to drugs, *Whatever.*
——John Kelly talking before Congress

Hold your babies, your loved ones, everyone very dear to you close. Life is so precious. It can change in an instant. There are things that will absolutely never make sense. Just know that life's too short for drama, the negativity! All the unnecessary! Cherish what you have and be forever grateful! Love with all your heart and never live with regret!!!
——My daughter's Facebook post

In a New York minute, everything can change.
——Eagles

The secret of change is to focus all of your energy not on fighting the old, but on building the new.
—Socrates

Silence is as good an answer as words. If you say how you feel and get no response, the lack of a response is your answer. Move on!
—Shilo

If someone threw a rock and knocked you off your donkey, would you be considered stoned off your ass?

Beer is living proof that God loves us and wants us to be happy.
—Ben Franklin

You have two ears and one mouth. Maybe you should listen more.
—Jacob, *Survivor*

*****

My granddaughter is like a corn field. She has *big ears*.

*****

What can you expect from a pig but a grunt.
—Gerrie

When you wrestle in the mud with a pig, you will never win. The pig gets dirty, but they like it.

*****

Life's too short. We become what we do. You need teamwork to make the dream work!

The only thing worse than training your employees and having them leave is not training them and having them stay.

—Henry Ford

If the facts are against you, pound the law. If the law is against you, pound the facts. If the law and the facts are against you, pound the table and yell a lot! If you are in a tough situation, have a positive attitude and ideas. You will be okay! Design is not just what it looks and feels like, design is how it works.

—Steve Jobs

Speak without offending. Listen without defending.

—Montel Williams

You have permission to *engage*!

—FlyGirl

Get Gutsy, live Gutsy.

—FlyGirl

There's a thousand reason why I shouldn't drink...but I can't think of one right now.

—Shemp Howard
(Samuel Horowitz, 1895–1955),
actor of the *Three Stooges* fame

Ask not what your country can do for you, ask what you can do for your country.
—John F. Kennedy

Change will not come, if we wait for some other person or some other time. We are the change that we seek.
—Barack Obama

Do I look like a guy who needs hookers?
—Donald Trump

*****

For a better digestion system, drink beer. If you lose your appetite, drink wine. If you have high blood pressure, drink scotch. If you have a cold, drink schnapps.

*****

Help is only helpful if it seems helpful by the person giving the help.

Everyone that enters this place makes us happy! Some when they arrive and some when they leave!

*****

Worrying is like paying a debt that may never come due.
—Will Rogers

Every day we prepare 5,000 plated meals for your consumption...
—Cruise ships

*****

You've got to let go and trust what is best for your life. It's hard to find healing when you are trying to find closure. You will drive yourself crazy for trying to understand their reasons.

*****

You have to expect things of yourself before you can do them.
—Michael Jordon

Don't piss off old people. It just means less time they will have to spend in prison!

You are not your illness. You have an individual story to tell. You have a name, a personality. Staying yourself is part of the battle.
—Julian Seifter

Mood disorders are terribly painful illnesses, and they are isolating illnesses. And they make people feel terrible about themselves when in fact, they can be treated.
—Kay Redfield Jamison

Mental illness is nothing to be ashamed of, but stigma and bias shame us all.
—Bill Clinton

There should be no shame in having a mental illness, but the stigma that individuals and their families feel far too often. What we all must come to understand is that essentially every one of us is affected by mental illness in some way, whether by living with an illness ourselves or

grappling with the consequences in a friend or loved one.
—Scott L. Rauch, MD

There is no health without mental health.
—David Satcher, MD, PhD

No one would ever say that someone with a broken arm or a broken leg is less than a whole person, but people will say that or imply that all the time about people with a mental illness.
—Elyn Saks

You can always extract the good from your mental illness.
—Unknown

If you can show compassion for your fears, you can begin to overcome them.
—Unknown

If you can face the worst fears your mind can create, you can overcome just about anything.
—Unknown

*****

In making others happy, you will be happy too. For the happiness you give away returns to shine on you.
—Helen Steiner Rice

*****

You have to practice like you're in second place, but play like you're a champion.

—Joe Beilein

The key is not the "will to win." Everybody has that. It is the will to prepare to win that is important.

—Bobby Knight

When opportunity comes, it's too late to prepare. Confidence comes from being prepared.

—John Wooden

It's harder to stay on the top than it is to make the climb. Continue to seek new goals.

—Pat Summit

It would not be much of a universe, if it wasn't home to the people you love.

—Stephen Hawking

If you're smoking in here, you better be on fire!

It's better to be pissed off than be pissed on. Unless you have a snakebite or you're on fire.

*****

If you have a reservation, you must be in the wrong place.

I would not become a member of a country club that would allow me to join.
—Groucho Marx

If dogs and cats don't go to heaven, I want to go where they go.

I asked the Lord to send me a dog. He sent me an angel.

Let me be the person my dog thinks I am.

Everybody should believe in something. I believe I'll have another beer.

Beer is the answer but I can't remember the question.

The beating will continue until the moral changes.

*****

In the mountains, we forget to count the days. At the lake, we forget to count the days.

Relax! You're at the cabin.

If you think you don't have any friends, just build a cabin in the mountains, or at a river, or lake.

This could be your new hospitality desk!

I named my dog Five Miles so I can tell people I walked five miles today.

*****

Cleaning and scrubbing can wait till tomorrow,
for babies grow up we've learned to our sorrow.
So quiet down the cobwebs; Dust go to sleep!
I'm rocking my baby, and babies don't keep.
—Unknown

*****

Golf isn't everything, but it sure beats *Whatever* is second.

One day at a time. This is enough. Do not look back and grieve over the past, for it is gone. And do not be troubled about the future, for it has not come. Live in the present and make it so beautiful that it will be worth remembering.

Camping without wine is just sitting in the woods.

Wine. Amazing how this simple, lovely liquid sinks in and smooths the soul.

Life is short. Eat dessert first. Life is short. Smile while you still have teeth. Life is short. Order the good wine!
—Glenn Frey

He stole her heart, so she stole his last name.

This house belongs to the cats. I'm just here to open the cans.

Loved you yesterday. Love you still. Always have. Always will.

If I give you a straw, will you suck the fun out of someone else's day?

*****

People don't care if your house is clean, they only care if you have wine!

I drink to make other people more interesting.

I'm outdoorsy. I like drinking on the porch.

*****

I love you for all that you are, all that you have been and all that you are yet to become.

From this day forward, you will not walk alone. May my heart be your shelter and my arms be your home.

*****

Advice from a mountain lion:

- Stand your ground.
- Put your best foot forward.
- Climb to new heights.
- Stay wild at heart.
- Always land on your feet.

*****

Advice from a trail:

- Stay on your path.
- Find inspiration around every turn.
- Tread lightly.

- Every day has its ups and downs.
- Watch your step.

*****

Advice from an elk:

- Appreciate life's high points.
- Don't get stuck in a rut.
- Cherish wide-open spaces.
- Make your voice heard.
- Be magnificent.

*****

Advice from a tree:

- Stand tall and proud.
- Sink your roots into the earth.
- Be content with your natural beauty.
- Drink plenty of water.
- Enjoy the view.

*****

Southerners are real hospital folks. They have a special way of talking. Who love soft breezes. A front porch with rocking chairs. Fishing, iced tea, fried chicken, and lazy Sunday afternoons. They love children, freshy baked apple pie, huntin' days, biscuits and gravy, and magnolias trees, good neighbors, and a friendly conversation.

ASAP (As Southern as Possible).

*****

Guest towels are to be used by guests. Nonguests will please dry their hands on their clothes.

Reality is an illusion caused by the lack of wine.

"Paddle faster, I hear banjos playing." Remember that one?

I'm not as thinked as you stoned I am.

*****

A drunk goes to court.
The judge says, "You've been brought here for drinking."
The drunk says. "Great, let's get started!"

Friends are God's way of apologizing for your family.
—Bob Dylan

Irish people never say goodbye when they leave, and Jewish people say goodbye but never leave.
—Mel Brooks

*****

Fight hard between the whistles, and after the whistle blows, focus hard on what you will do between the next set of whistles!

*****

Great leaders are almost always great simplifiers, who can cut through argument, debate
and doubt, to offer a solution everybody can
understand.

—Colin Powell

We're happy to share with you such as we've got:
the leaks in our roof and the soup in the pot.

*****

Six months ago, I couldn't even spel salezmun, now I are one!

*****

Music is the highest form of expression we have
as humans. This museum so beautifully embodies that spirit.

—Andy Summers of Police

The MIM (Musical Instrument Museum) in Phoenix

The doors

*****

I believe that the doors and this type of architecture of some of the houses and areas now in Italy and other countries were built so big so as to allow them to ride on their horses and carriages into the courtyards.

> If the doors of perception were cleansed, everything would appear to man as it is, infinite. For man has closed himself up till he sees all things through narrow chinks of his cavern.
>
> —William Blake

This book, *The Doors of Perception*, is where Jim Morrison got his inspiration to name his band the Doors! The summer of 1965, The Doors were born.

Shirt worn by Jim Morrison of the Doors (1969). Phoenix Arizona. (I know this because my friend Joanne C. made spaghetti dinner for him at her house. And he left his shirt there.)

Poster in Paris

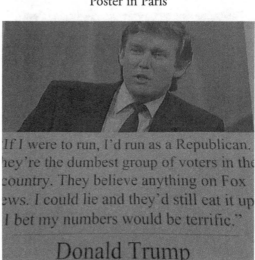

Whose home? I think the lights are on but is anybody home!!!!

Being drunk is a good disguise. I drink so I can
talk to a——holes. This includes myself.
                                    —Rodney Dangerfield

*****

Oh, how things can change in twenty years.
Let your past make you better, not bitter!!!

Eileen

Technically, Moses was the first person with a tablet, download-ing data from the cloud.

Dinner choices:

We don't eat dairy, meat, soy, gluten, eggs, or nuts.
What do you recommend we get?
Get out!

*****

When you make a big change to your life, it is
really scary. What is scarier is having regrets.

Go ahead. Make my day!
— Clint Eastwood, *Sudden Impact* (1983)

Happiness can be found in the darkest of times,
if one only remembers to turn on the light.
— Harry Potter (2004)

Toto, I've got feeling we are not Kansas anymore.
— Dorothy Gale,
The Wizard of OZ (1939)

Here's looking at you, kid.
— Rick Blaine, *Casablanca* (1942)

*****

Sometimes you just have to let go and trust what's best for your life.
It is hard to find healing when you are trying to find closure. You will
go nuts trying to find any understanding for their reasoning.
Remember, everybody doesn't think the same!

*****

If you have to ask if it's too early to drink wine, you're an amateur and we can't be friends!

If Target had a bar, my life would be perfect!

Tell me and I'll forget. Teach me and I'll remember. Involve me and I'll learn.

—Ben Franklin

*****

John Lennon piano. MIM (Musical Instrument Museum)

Beatles traveling exhibit

Sometimes you just have to put yourself on a time-out!

*****

I am still determined to be cheerful and happy, in a *Whatever situation* I may be in, for I have also learned from experience that the greater part of happiness or misery depends upon our dispositions and not upon our circumstances.
—Martha Washington

What do women do after sex?
2% eat,
3% smoke,
4% sleep,
5% take a shower,
86% finish the job themselves!

Orgasms are good for your health! They can lower a women's risk of heart disease, stroke, breast cancer, and depression. So have sex and get healthy...
—Pure Romance

There are four seasons: winter, spring, summer, football!

One must always aim beyond the target; one must aim a long way. Our whole life, our whole spirit travels with the arrow. And when the arrow has been released, it is never the end.
—Awa Kenzo

Blessed are the hairstylists, for they bring out the beauty in others!

*****

T-shirt in LA. Not sold in St. Louis

Hoodoo: "You-Doo"

Yum yum!

*****

Sometimes we are limited more by our attitude than by opportunities.

—Unknown

There are no menial jobs, only menial attitudes.

—William John Bennett

It's not the position, but the disposition.

—J. E. Dinger

*****

You've got to let go and trust. It's best for life.

It's hard to find healing when you're trying hard to find closure. You will drive yourself crazy trying to find understanding for their reason.

Sometimes you just need to tell yourself "People just don't think the same." Say that and move on!

Or you can say BOHICA. Bend Over Here It Comes Again. And just move on.

*****

When I was five years old, my mother told me that happiness was the key to a good life. When I went to school, my teacher asked me what I wanted to be when I grew up. I said happy. They told me that I didn't understand the assignment, and I told my teacher they didn't understand life.

*****

A possible story of how the card game, Texas Hold 'Em, started. Cowboys in Texas in the mid-1800s invented the game so more people could play at one time. Not sure if this is true but I'm going with it until I am told something different.

*****

I didn't think you had an ace but *Whatever.*
—Daniel Negreanu

Winners tell jokes, losers say deal. We cannot change the cards we are dealt, just the way we play the hand. If you play the right hands, you will win. Now that's a profound statement.

If you can't recognize the sucker at the table, it must be you.

What is luck? When preparedness meets opportunity! The opportunity was there, and you were prepared to take it.

Waiting to see her teacher.

Teachers shape the future one child at a time!

So well respected even more now, after doing some homeschooling.

Teacher arrives

Everyone who remembers his own education remembers teachers, not methods and techniques. The teacher is the heart of the educational system.

The dreams that you dare to dream really do come true.

—First Man

Having someone who gets you and how you are feeling even before you feel it. That's true love.

—Christian, *Survivor*

Hatred corrodes the container it's carried in.

I shall study and prepare myself so when my chance comes, I will be ready.

—Abe Lincoln

Perfection is the enemy of profitability.

—Mark Cuban

We have one very powerful business rule. It is concentrated in one word: courtesy!

—Henry Wells (1864), businessman and Wells Fargo founder

You can't grow old playing games, you grow old from not playing.

Make a difference today for someone who is fighting for tomorrow.

—Jim Kelly

Shoot for the moon, even if you miss. You'll land among the stars…

—Unknown

Go confidently in the direction of your dreams! Live the life you've imagined.

—Thoreau

*****

Today is our greatest adventure. Make it count!
Believe in your dreams.

ROV, to purposefully journey without a definite plan.

FIAT (Fix It Again Tony)

I wish retail therapy was covered by my health insurance. Happy holidays.

Teens would rather text then talk.

*****

It's not about where you have been, it's about where you end up and how much distance you have covered.

—Matt Higgins

Keep your face to the sunshine and you never see the shadows.

—Helen Keller

If you can dream it, you can do it.

—Walt Disney

Coming together is a beginning, keeping together is progress, working together is success.

—Edward Everett Hale

Nothing is softer or more flexible than water, yet nothing can resist it.

—Lao-tzu

You can do what you have to do, and sometimes you can do it even better than you think you can.

—Jimmy Carter

Have confidence in everything. No matter what it is that you're doing, know that you can do it better than anyone.

—O'Shea Jackson Jr.

Once you win, you have no doubt that everyone has a part to play. We have the power. You can do it.

—Maxine Waters

Nothing is impossible. The word itself says "I'm possible!"

—Audrey Hepburn

I never dreamt of success. I worked for it.

—Estée Lauder

Can't change the direction of the wind, but I can adjust my sails to always reach my destination.

—Jimmy Dean

Always bear in mind that your own resolution to succeed is more important than any other one thing.

—Abraham Lincoln

*****

ATTITUDE

The longer I live, the more I realize the impact of attitude on life. Attitude, to me, is more important than facts. It is more important than the past, education, the money, the circumstances, than failure, than success, that what other people think or say or do. It is more important than appearance, giftedness, or skill. It will make or break a company...a church...a home. The remarkable thing is we have a choice every day regarding the attitude we will embrace for that day. We cannot change our past. We cannot change the fact that people will act in a certain way. We cannot change the inevitable. The only thing we can do is play on the one string we have, and that is our attitude. I am convinced that life is 10% of what happens to me and 90% of how I react to it. And so it is with you. We are in charge of our attitudes.

—Charles R. Swindoll

It's great to be a champion. You must believe you are the best. If you are not, pretend you are.

—Muhammad Ali

It's not what happens to you that determines how far you will go in life, it is how you handle what happens to you.

—Zig Ziglar

Everyone has a burden. What counts is how you carry it.

—Merle Miller

The state of your life is nothing more than a reflection of your state of mind.

—Dr. Wayne W. Dryer

Ability is what you are capable of doing. Motivation determines what you do. Attitude determines how well you do it.

—Lou Holtz

The optimist sees opportunity in every danger. The pessimist sees danger in every opportunity.

—Winston Churchill

Positive thinking won't let you do anything, but it will let you do everything better than negative thinking will.

—Zig Ziglar

Minds are like parachutes. They only function when open.

—Thomas Dewar

Holding on to anger is like grasping a hot coal with the intent of throwing it at someone else. You are the one who gets burned.

—Buddha

Eagles come in all shapes and sizes, but you can recognize them chiefly by their attitudes.
—Charles Prestwich Scott

To be a great champion, you must believe you are the best. If you're not, pretend you are.
—Muhammad Ali

A man without a smiling face must not open shop.
—Chinese proverb

A healthy attitude is contagious but don't wait to catch it from others. Be a carrier.
—Unknown

Attitude determines altitude.
—Unknown

People who say it cannot be done should not interrupt those who are doing it.
—Unknown

The control center of your life is your attitude.
—Unknown

There are no menial jobs, only menial attitudes.
—William John Bennett

It's not the situation. It's your reaction to the situation.
—Robert Conklin

It's not the position but the disposition.
—J. E. Dinger

I never saw a pessimistic general win a battle.
—General Dwight David Eisenhower

When you choose to be unpleasant and positive in the way you treat others, you have also chosen, in most cases, how you are going to treat others.
—Zig Ziglar

The only disabled in life is a bad attitude.
—Scott Hamilton

You can disagree without being disagreeable.
—Zig Ziglar

Funny is an attitude.
—Flip Wilson

Things turn out the best for the people who make the best of the way things turn out.
—John Wooden

Whatever is expressed is impressed. *Whatever* you say to yourself, with emotion, generates thoughts, ideas, and behaviors with those words.
—Brian Tracy

When you believe you can, you can!
—Maxwell Maltz

*****

Observation becomes participation.
Choreograph your experiences.
Our world is a canvas to your imagination.

If you create the stage and it is grand, everyone who enters will play his part.
Transfer intense anticipation into reality.

*****

Golf is a game in which attitude of the mind counts for more than mightiness of muscle.
—Arnold Haultin (1908)

If my mind can conceive it and I can believe it, I can achieve it.
—Larry Holmes

Golf is 90% mental.
—Jack Nicklaus

If you don't read the newspaper, you are uninformed. If you read the newspaper, you are misinformed.
—Mark Twain

The truth is not always the truth.
—Rudy Giuliani

I don't make jokes. I just watch the government and report the facts.
—Will Rogers
(Wait, when did he say this?)

Talk is cheap…except when the government does it.
—Unknown

A government big enough to give you everything you want, is strong enough to take everything you have.

—Thomas Jefferson

Who knew that even so far back in history, it's still the same?

*****

I am a firm believer in the people. If given the truth, they can be depended upon to meet any national crises. The great point is to bring them the real facts.

—Abraham Lincoln

Get your facts first, then you can distort them as you please.

—Mark Twain

Never miss a good chance to shut up.

—Will Rogers

Never let yesterday use up too much of today.

—Will Rogers

"We think that she finds the idol she'll have to play it before the merge. We'd like to get it back."
"*Whatever.*"

—Sugar, *Survivor*

*****

If you had purchased $1,000.00 of Delta Air Line stock one year ago, you would have $49.00 left. With Enron, you would have had

$16.50 left of the original $1,000.00. With WorldCom, you would have had less than $5.00 left.

But if you had purchased $1,000.00 worth of beer one year ago, drank all the beer, and turned in all the cans for the aluminum recycling refund, you would have $214.00 in cash.

Based on the information above, the best current investment advice is to drink heavily and recycle. It's called the 401-Keg.

*****

Finish each day and be done with it. You have done what you could. Some blunders and absurdities no doubt crept in. Forget them as soon as you can. Tomorrow is a new day. Begin it well and serenely and with too high a spirit to be cumbered with your old nonsense.

—Ralph Waldo Emerson

A sign is an invitation to buy but not a contract to sell. How many times have you run into this? It is important that we all just get along.

—Retail sign

No, you want me to do it. *Whatever.*

—*Amazing Race.*

I'd kill a snitch. I can't say I have and not saying I haven't, *Whatever.*

—Peyton Manning

You have to take care of tomorrow, as today will take care of itself.

It's all about presentation. We've been saying that all year, whether how you frame a pitch or *Whatever.*

—Harold Reynolds

"So you are Jason Hanky's supervisor?"
"Sponsor."
"*Whatever.*"

—George

The flowers are wilted but the memories will last forever. Happiness is the not the absence of stress. It's the ability to cope with it.

Even if you are on the right track, you will get run over if you just sit there.

—Will Rogers

*****

Latitude. *Whatever*
Longitude. Who cares? Glacier National Park

*****

Did you get a haircut? No, I got them all cut. First time you heard that today?

*****

Life without passion. You're dead.

—Shirley Schmidt

You're not as young as you use to be, but not as old as you're going to be.

"Footwear needed for the WSOP (World Series of Poker). Loafers, flip flops, sneakers, *Whatever.*" That about sums it up!

Once you let your grief become anger, it will never go away.

—*Lost*

A generation that commences a revolution can rarely complete it.

—Thomas Jefferson

*****

You can't come back unless you leave.

—Robert De Niro

Remember, everyone doesn't think the same.

You learn a lot of what not to do from other people.

Don't look at others to see what they are doing wrong. Look to see what they are doing right. Maybe you will be able to use some of their ways and incorporate them into your ways.

Flattery is one of the highest compliments.

*****

If you unconsciously live a conscious life, you can never be poor.

—Chinese proverb

You'll be free to do *Whatever.*

—*Boston Legal*

*****

Relationships start with a single date.

Do unto your friends and others as you would have them do unto you. You should have, and we all should have do unto other friends.

*****

Everyone knows how the puzzle was laid but can anyone recall the solution?
—*Tarkio Road*,
Brewer & Shipley from the 60s

The times… They are a-changin'.
—Bob Dylan (1964) (So true then and so true now.)

"Make love not war." (What happened to the sixties?)

Peace sign hanging in the Smithsonian Institute.

When the power of love overcomes the love of power, the world will know peace.

—Indian proverb

*****

It's not where you start but where you end up that counts. Hopefully we will all end up in the right place.

Stepping over dollars to pick up pennies. Never mix profit with a prophet.

*****

Memo from Herb:

Your generous allowance of time is greatly appreciated. I am sure your decision not to buy my very fine merchandise is based on careful consideration...you dumb SOB.

Doing business with you is like wearing a condom. It gives one the feeling of faith, security, and safety while getting screwed!

*****

The ability to control thought process, to concentrate on a task, is almost universally recognized as the most important key to effective performance in sport.

—Unknown

It's not a question of getting rid of the butterflies. It is a question of getting them to fly in formation.

—Jack Donohue,
Olympic basketball coach

Today's goals are tomorrow realities.

—Terry Orlick

People are just about as happy as they make their minds up to be.

—Abe Lincoln

"We work like a duck in water, calm to the public eye but paddling and working like crazy under water where you cannot be seen."

"Success or failure in business is caused more by mental attitude than by mental capacities."

—Sir Walter Scott

Our attitude toward life determines life's attitude toward us.

—Earl Nightingale

Those who dare to fail miserably can achieve greatness.

—John F. Kennedy

There are 86,400 seconds in a day. Make them all work for you.

Never let a fool kiss you or for you to kiss a fool.

A woman who strives to be like a man lacks ambition.

If you are not part of the solution, then you are part of the problem.

—DJ

Forty games in forty nights. *Whatever*. Let's get it going.

—Doug Collins

Win or lose or *Whatever*, you have to learn to take the shot.

—Doug Collins

The last game we beat them by *Whatever*.

—Phil Jackson

It's the seventh or eighth or *Whatever*. Get the ball to Mariano Rivera.

—Announcer

I have to make a birdie somewhere. I don't care if I finish twentieth or thirtieth *Whatever*.

—Bernard Langer

Your own mind is a sacred enclosure into which nothing harmful can enter except by your permission.

—Ralph Waldo Emmerson

We are the people our parents warned us about.

—Jimmy Buffett

I am always the one to step up, *Whatever*.

—Melisa, *The Apprentice*

I want to get started on the right foot with her. I don't want to make the same mistake I made with Alan's wife, Julie, Judith or *Whatever*.

—*Two and a Half Men*

Don't take anything personally. Nothing others do is because of you. What others say and do is a projection of their own reality, their own dream. When you're immune to the opinions and actions of others, you won't be the victim of needless suffering.

—Don Miguel Ruiz

*****

Sometimes I hold myself from urinating for a long time, so when I go, it feels like I am having an orgasm.

If there weren't some bumps in your work then they wouldn't need you.

*****

Some days, doing "the best we can" may still fall short of what we would like to be able to do, but life isn't perfect on any front, and doing what we can with what we have is the most we should expect of ourselves or anyone else.

—Fred Rogers

*****

A great way to start your day!

*****

The only person you should try to be better than
is the person you were yesterday.

*****

Ten Commandments For Communicating Successfully
with Persons Affected by Hearing Loss:

1. Thou shalt not speak from another room.
2. Thou shalt not speak with your back toward the person
    with hearing loss.
3. Thou shalt not start speaking and then turn away from the
    person with hearing loss.
4. Thou shalt not speak in competition with anything else,
    i.e., mute the TV, turn off running water, move to a quieter
    environment, etc.

5. Thou shalt get the attention of the person with the hearing loss before you begin speaking, i.e., say their name and pause.
6. Thou shalt speak face to face when possible.
7. Thou shalt try to remove obstructions while speaking such as your hand in front of your mouth, food in your mouth, etc.
8. Thou shalt speak clearly and distinctly. Project and enunciate.
9. Thou shalt exercise patience with communicating.
10. Thou shalt be supportive to the person with hearing loss.

I'm just saying!

*****

Love is patient, love is kind
Love always protects, always trusts, always hopes,
always preserves.
Love never fails. (1 Corinthians 13)

*****

Pong was one of the first video games invented.
Pong was originally invented as a warm-up exercise.

*****

Event planner: someone who does precision work based on unreliable data by those who can't make up their mind. See also wizard, magician.

Thank you for you service and for your sacrifice!!!

Your job is not to die for your country. It's to make the other bastard die for his.
—General George S. Patton

Lead me, follow me, or get out of my way.
—General George S. Patton

Till everyone comes home, till the battle ends. Everyone is safe with their family and friends. Then we shall have peace.

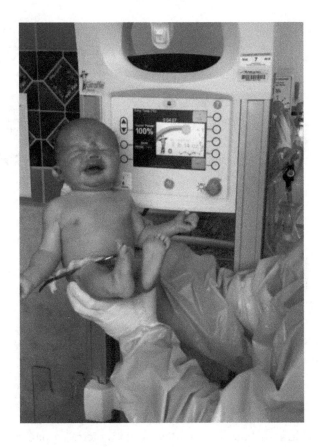

And so, it begins

I don't like sitting around doing nothing, as I do
not know when I am finished.

—Rich Little

Read the f——king manual

*****

The bigger the dream, the more important the team.

Teamwork makes dreams work!

Good instincts usually tell you what to do before your head has figured it out.

*****

Human Freedom involves our capacity to pause between stimulus and response and, in that pause, to choose the one response toward which we wish to throw our weight. The capacity to create ourselves, based upon this freedom, is inseparable from consciousness or self-awareness.

—Rollo May

A friend is someone who knows all about you and still loves you.

—Mark Twain

Better to have it and not need it than to not have it and need it.

A positive attitude may not solve all your problems. But it will annoy enough people to make it worth the effort.

*****

Make sure you make the book for the reader and not the writer. This one is for both.

*****

Take care of the little things, and the big things will take care of themselves.
—Jeff Saturday

Clint Eastwood said, "Improvise, Adapt, Overcome." Now a Marine's slogan from the movie *Heartbreak Ridge*.

You don't have losses you, only have lessons.
—Sean McVay

You can't have someone beat if you go out.

It's simple. Do what you want to do. If you don't want to do it, forget it. But if you do want to do it, get out of my —— way.
—Willie Nelson

Friendship doubles our joy and divides our sorrow.

The light of love to live by, the wine of friendship for sharing, the bread of peace to nourish heart and for these we give thanks each day.

Leadership consists of nothing less than taking responsibility for everything that goes wrong and giving your subordinates credit for everything that goes well.

—Dwight D. Eisenhower

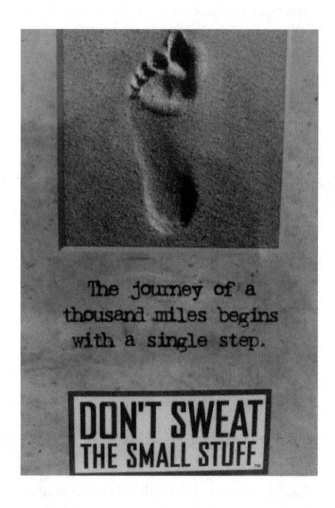

Gratitude is not only the greatest of virtues, but the parent of all others. Enthusiasm, laughter, and a smile are contagious. Not having enthusiasm, laughter, and a smile is also contagagious.

Life is not a fairy tale. If you lose a shoe at midnight, you are not a princess, you're drunk.

Boredom is a lack of productivity.

My wife asked me to take her to one of those restaurants where they make the food in front of you. I took her to Subway. That's how the fight started.

Golf in Florida may be a little different!!!

*****

Adapt to the circumstances in order to make progress.
    To golf or not to golf? What a silly question!

*****

Therapist said, "Your wife says you never buy her flowers. Is that true?"
    To be honest, I never knew she sold flowers.

*****

Confuse your doctor by putting on rubber gloves the same time he does!

*****

When I donate blood, I don't extract it myself. The nurse does it for me.

"I don't think you understand. This is a sperm bank, and things don't operate that way here."

*****

I picked up a hitchhiker. Seemed like a nice guy.

After a few miles, he asked me if I wasn't afraid that he might be a serial killer. I told him the odds of two serial killers in the same car were extremely unlikely.

*****

A man asked his wife what she would do if he won the lottery.

She replied, "I'd take half and leave you."

"Great," he said. "I won $4, here's $2. Stay in touch."

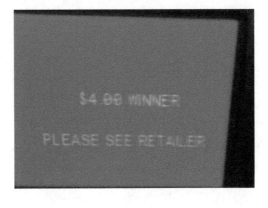

*****

I don't think the therapist is supposed to say "wow" that many times in your first session. But here we are.

*****

I asked my grandpa, "How come after so many years, you still call Grandma sweetie, honey, darling? What's the secret?"

He said, "I forgot her name five years ago and I was afraid to ask her."

*****

Sobbing my heart out, eyes swollen, nose red, I say, "I can't see you anymore. I am not going to let you hurt me again like you just did."

"It was a sit-up. You did one sit-up," the trainer replies.

*****

Sex after surgery.

A recent article states that a man has sued the local hospital, saying that after his wife had surgery there, she lost all interest in sex.

The hospital replied that his wife had come in for cataract surgery. "All we did was correct her eyesight."

*****

The three hardest things to say:

1. "I was wrong."
2. "I made a mistake."
3. "Worcestershire sauce."

*****

"I told my wife I wanted to be cremated. She made an appointment for me Tuesday."
—Rodney Dangerfield

*****

A daughter is…a joy bringer, a heart warmer, a memory maker. A daughter is love.

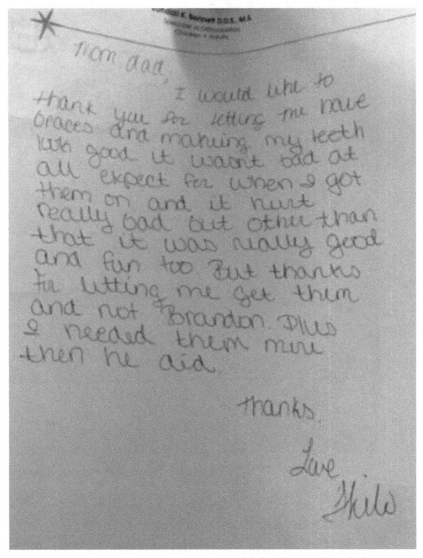

A nice note from an eleven-year-old daughter to her dad.

*****

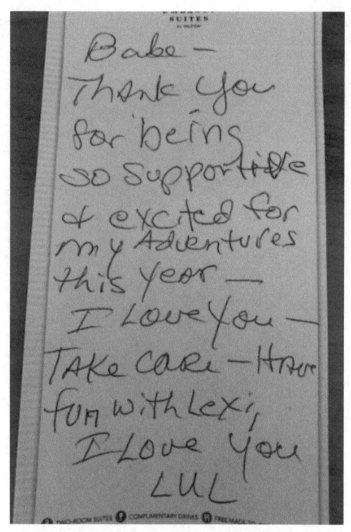

A nice note from his wife!

Remember to be supportive of others. Sometimes it is not your turn to go. You may go another time or not at all.

Be a support and be happy for someone else. It just may not be your turn.

Help someone when you can!!! Don't hit or talk badly about people. There is not a time in your life when that will help.

How many words did you know?

*****

Friendship is when people know all about you, but they love you anyway.

It' s five o'clock somewhere!!!

I drank so much tonight. I may have to sleep in the bathtub!

I'm giving up drinking for a month. Sorry. Bad punctuation. I'm giving up. Drinking for a month.

I went line dancing last night. Well, it was a roadside sobriety test.

Hangover: just God's way of saying you kicked ass last night.

*****

HOW TO PEE
WITH MORNING WOOD

THE TUBE

THE SUPERMAN

THE HANDSTAND

THE FROG

THE LUNGE

THE BLOW DRYER

Keep yourself healthy! Drink water, eat healthy, and sleep. Your life will be so much better if you stay healthy!

*****

Always be honest. Lying always will get you in trouble, and one lie leads to another lie to another.

No one is perfect, as long as you did your best. At least you tried.

Please, please say please and thank you all the time, and also mean it when you do.

Have a magical day!

*****

When talking to someone, look them in the eye. Be a good listener. It is not your time to talk. Let them talk and then you will have your turn. No matter what they say, it will remind you of something that may have happened to you or a situation you know of. Don't interrupt and let them talk and be a good listener. You can talk afterward. Be attentive to them. Think before you speak. Let them have the stage for now, and you will get your turn.

Remember when all is bad and you feel that everything is coming down around you, stay positive. You will always have your family. Friends may come and go and relationships may come and go, but you will always have your family. New friends are great, but old friends know where you have been. Cherish family and friends, and don't forget it!!! There isn't anything you can do that will make your family stop loving you.

If you don't get it right the first time, try again and again if needed. Don't get discouraged. Giving up is the only way to fail.

Challenge yourself. Challenge yourself to make things better.

Homework is not supposed to be easy. Hard work and doing your homework will make you smarter and you will enjoy your life more.

*****

This picture was taken by three girls having fun at a bar.
There are three ladies and who or what is the fourth head.
This picture has not been altered or photoshopped.

*****

Be thankful for what you have and not unthankful for what you don't have.

Don't be afraid to ask a question. No question is stupid, and the only stupid question is the one that is not asked, but sometimes you may not get the answer you want.

At times, learn what not to do from other people.

Don't look at the faults of things. Look at what is being done right. I don't care what they are doing wrong. I want to know what they are doing right.

Always be the best you can be, and do the best you can. You don't have to win all the time. If you win, then someone else loses, and that is not good for them. At least you played. Do your best, and then you will know that you tried. Maybe they were better than you this time, and you can learn from that.

Don't let others pressure you into doing things. Mom would say if the other kids jumped off the bridge, would you also?

Learn to have good manners. It is important how you carry yourself and your personality. Make good manners a habit.

If you give a smile, you will get a smile back. The universal language is laughter and a smile. If you use this, you will get along with everyone.

The good vibes that you give off can attract other good vibes coming your way.

You make the call

*****

Stay active, exercise, walk and drink water. Get into the habit of being active. Your muscles were given to you to be used.

Have a hobby. Do something that you like, not because you have to but because you want to.

The only things you have to do is pay taxes and die.

*****

I believe churches are meant for praising God.
But so are the 2 a.m. car rides, showers, coffee shops, the gym, conversations with friends,
strangers, etc. Don't let a building confine your
faith because we will never change the world by
just going to church. We need to be the church.

—Unknown

*****

In the blink of an eye, everything can change.

As the Eagles said, "In a New York Minute, everything can
change." So forgive all and love with all your heart. You may never
know when you may need that chance again.

*****

Keep life moving forward. Looking backwards is
only for time travelers.

—Rachel O.

Don't stop until you're proud.

—Unknown

If you lie down at night, knowing in your heart
that made someone's day a little better, you know
than you had a good day!

Throw kindness around like confetti!

—Molly B.

After every storm there's a rainbow, no matter how long it takes to show up.

If you follow the herd, you will never be heard.

—Norah, *Survivor*

*****

Person at the pharmacy asks, "What are the side effect of this drug?" Pharmacist answers, "Bankruptcy!"

*****

One of the biggest lies I tell myself is "I don't need to write it down, I'll remember it."

*****

I asked my granddaughter to get me the newspaper.

She laughed and said, "Granddaddy, you are old. Just use my phone."

So I used her phone to kill the big spider.

*****

Life is all about ass.

You are either covering it, laughing it off, kicking it, kissing it, busting it, trying to get a piece of it. Or behaving like one. Or you live with one.

*****

In this family, we do second chances. We do grace, we do real, we do prayers. We do mistakes, we do I'm sorrys. We do loud really well, and we do hugs.

We do family.
We do love.

*****

If everyone is moving forward together, then success takes care of itself.

—Henry Ford

The greatest discovery of all time is that a person can change his future by merely changing his attitude.

—Oprah Winfrey

Alone we can do so little, together we can do so much.

—Helen Keller

Individual commitment to a group effort—that is what makes a team work, a company work, a society work, a civilization work.

—Vince Lombardi

Talent wins games, but teamwork and intelligence win championships.

—Michael Jordan

If you want to improve yourself, the organization gets pulled up with you.

Because you're mine, I walk the line.

—Johnny Cash

It's unbelievable how much you don't know about the game you've been playing all your life.

—Mickey Mantle

Give me six hours to chop down a tree and I'll spend the first four sharpening my ax.

—Abe Lincoln

*****

Groundhog Day

On this day in 1887, Groundhog Day, featuring a rodent meteoroligist, is celebrated for the first time at Gobbler's Knob in Punxsutawney, Pennsylvania. According to tradition, if the groundhog comes out of his hole on this day and sees its shadow, there will be six more weeks of winter weather. No shadow means an early spring.

Groundhog day has its roots in ancient Christian tradition of Candlemas Day, when clergy would bless and distribute candles needed for winter. The candles represent how long and cold the winter would be. Germans expanded on this concept by selecting an animal—the hedgehog—as the means for predicting weather.

Once they came to America, German settlers in Pennsylviana continued the tradition, although they switched from hedgehogs to groundhogs, which were more plentiful in the United States.

Groundhogs, also called woodchucks and whose scientific name is *Marmota monax*, typically weigh twelve to fifteen pounds and live from six to eight years. They eat vegetables and fruits, whistle when they are frightned or looking for a mate, and can climb trees and swim. They go into hibernation in late fall during this time. Their body tempertures drop significally. Their heartbeat drop from eighty to five beats per minute, and they can lose 30% of their body fat. In February, male groundhogs emerge form their burrows to look for a mate and not to predict the weather before goimg underground again. They come out of hibernation for good in March.

*****

Wishing you a happy *Whatever*. (I hope this doesn't offend you.)

*****

I sued the airlines for losing my luggage. I lost my case.

*****

I closed my eyes for but a moment and suddenly a man stood where my boy use to be. I may not be able now to carry you in my arms, but I will always carry you in my heart. You have given me so many reasons to be proud of the man you have become, but the proudest moment for me is telling others you are my son. I love you now and forever.

—Unknown

*****

My wife is still so hot! It just comes in flashes now.

*****

My wife got a job at the zoo. She's a keeper.

*****

A police toilet was stolen, and now the police have nothing to go on.

*****

Remain Hopeful!

Hope is an attitude. It is a mental shift that we choose for ourselves as we tap into our inner reserves. When we decide to be hopeful, we open ourselves to discover the wisdom and strength we may not have known existed. When we ask ourselves to stay positive and we answer the call, we are rewarded with the knowledge of what we have learned in life.

Our lessons, when viewed from this perspective, show us that things generally work out as they should. With hindsight, we are able to understand how a greater plan has been working in our lives.

Hope is a gift we can give to others as we encourage their dreams, comfort their sorrows, and remind them that the miracles are before us every day.

The most important thing is that though the process is called "the game of life" (by some), you always strive to do your best. When you come from this place known as "intention," your dreams begin to unfold before you. Possibilities you never imagined appear, and because you are sharing your best self, you are shown the gifts you have to share. When you learn to accept all that has happened along the way as necessary for your understanding, you will be able to view your life without regrets.

*****

Women need to follow their gut. *Whatever* your gut tells you. The very first thing. Sometimes women overanalyze things in making decisions, and I have thought that to be throughout my career that whenever I go with my gut, it's always the right choice.
—Gretchen Carlson, journalist, author

This could apply to men also as well as most everyone!

I didn't know that people talked with an accent until I left town.

*****

If you educate a child, you change their life. If you inspire a child, you can completely change the world!
—Mark Del Rosso, CEO,
Genesis Motor America

Remember, at times, the more eyes that look at it, the better off you may be. Don't be afraid to ask for some help.

Lake McDonald in Glacier National Park.
Lake McDonald. You need to go!!!

Glacier National Park, you need to see soon. By the year 2030, there could possibly be no more glaciers in Glacier National Park. It's not too cold, you just need to put more clothes on.

*****

April Fools' Day has been canceled this year, as no made-up prank can match the unbelievable stuff happening in the world right now.

*****

Sometimes you think things are falling apart, and only to find out they are falling into place.
—Unknown

You will never go broke taking a positive!
Wine...
Because it isn't good to keep things bottled up.

*****

FORGIVENESS

Anyone can hold a grudge, but it takes a person with character to forgive. When you forgive, you release yourself from a terrible burden.

Forgiveness doesn't mean what happened was okay, and it doesn't mean the person should still welcome you into your life. It just means you have made peace with the pain and are ready to let it go.

—Doe Zantamata

Well-behaved women rarely make history.
—Laurel Ulrich

I cook with wine, and sometimes I ever add the food.
—W. C. Fields

Everybody needs to be somewhere, so I chose a place with some class! A nice place to be. Do you wish you were here? Well make it happen!!!

*****

Grandparents' rules begin here, parents' rules end here.

—Sign on a floor entry mat

It's a goat my Lord in a flatbed ford, slowin down to take a look at me....

Beauty lay not in the thing, but in what the thing symbolized.

—Thomas Hardy

Give us your tired and weak / And we will make them strong / Bring us your foreign songs / And we will sing along. / Leave us your broken dreams / We'll give them time to mend. / There's still a lot of love / Living in the Promise land.
> —Willie Nelson

*****

You are holding a cup of coffee when someone comes along and bumps into you or shakes your arm, making you spill your coffee everywhere.

Why did you spill the coffee?

"Because someone bumped into me!"

Wrong answer.

You spilled the coffee because there was coffee in your cup. Had there been tea in the cup, you would have spilled tea.

Whatever is inside the cup is what will spill out. Therefore when life comes along and shakes you (which *will* happen), *Whatever* is inside you will come out. It's easy to fake it until you get rattled.

So we have to ask ourselves, "What's in my cup?"

When life gets tough, what spills over? Joy, gratefulness, peace, and humility? Anger, bitterness, harsh words, and reactions?

Life provides the cup. You choose how to fill it.

Today, let's work toward filling our cups with gratitude, forgiveness, joy, words of affirmation, and kindness, gentleness, and love for others.

*****

Some studies show that vegetarians are more likely to be depressed then meat-eaters (*Psychology Today*, Cornell University).

*****

You are braver than you believe, stronger than you seem, and smarter than you think.

—A. A. Milne

Is this the end?

Or are these the ends? But only the beginning?

Whatevah!!!

After Thoughts

Thank you for taking your time to read *Whatever*. I sure hope you enjoyed reading it as much as I enjoyed writing it.

Whatever was written for you in mind. You probably read some things you had already heard before and others you may not have and said to yourself, "I didn't know that. Oh, is that so?" That's great. And now you have had a few smiles and seen some new *Whatever* that will hopefully enhance your life as well as the lives of others. This could be a great reminder that we all need to walk the talk more often. It is my wish for you to use what you have read to engage with people differently when appropriate. Show more empathy toward them and also toward yourself. Remember to do your daily maintenance. When you help someone else, you also help yourself. Anticipate the needs of others. It's the little things that can make a big difference.

For a lifetime, I would see and hear *Whatever* everywhere—social media, TV, movies, books, friends, and family. There are so many positive thoughts and uplifting quotes and stories I could not capture them all. Now it is up to you to find your own *Whatever* to use them and create your own *Whatever* experiences and pass them on. Enrich your life as well as lives of others, and keep up your good attitude and sense of humor.

Remember as they say on an airplane to secure your own oxygen first in life! And don't forget to enjoy it!

About the Author

Mike is just a regular guy getting through this life that we all are trying to do. He is very much a people person and looks out for the betterment of others. Mike was in retail management for twenty years. Management is "getting work done through others." Adopting this philosophy at a young age of twenty, Mike began managing people almost all several years older. By his "WE" attitude and training skills, he was able to have a successful career in retail management. After retail, Mike became his own boss, doing a variety of work in the service industry. Self-employed for over thirty years now, he has been able to find work for himself and his friends, allowing him to keep up with bills and his parenting responsibilities. The scope of

Mike's many services offered within his business has provided him with a good life and many opportunities to travel domestically and abroad, for both work and pleasure. While working on-site logistics for large and small meetings and events, he has a large extended family all around the world. He sees and experiences *Whatever* all around him. Mike has been his own boss for over thirty years and has been collecting and documenting *Whatever* all around the world to now share with you.

Mike has two children and three grandchildren. Mike has been married now to Joy for two years. Joy and Mike danced together in the seventh grade, in Phoenix Arizona, and went to high school together but did not date. They accidentally met over fifty years later and fell in love.

CPSIA information can be obtained
at www.ICGtesting.com
Printed in the USA
LVHW081501121221
705996LV00009B/202